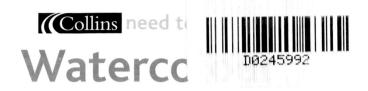

Collins need to

Waterco

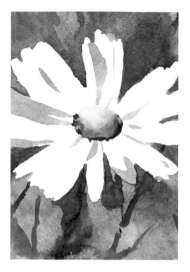

Collins need to know?

Watercolour

All the kit, techniques and inspiration
you need to get into painting

Alwyn Crawshaw • **June Crawshaw** • **Trevor Waugh**

First published in 2004 by
Collins, an imprint of
HarperCollins*Publishers*
77-85 Fulham Palace Road
Hammersmith, London W6 8JB

The Collins website address is:
www.collins.co.uk

Collins is a registered trademark of HarperCollins Publishers Limited.

08 07 06 05 04
6 5 4 3 2 1

A catalogue record for this book is available from the British Library

Created by: SP Creative Design
Editor: Heather Thomas
Designer: Rolando Ugolini
Cover design: Cook Design
Cover illustrations: Trevor Waugh

ISBN 0 00 718032 2

Originally published by Collins as:
You Can Paint Landscapes in Watercolour, 2003
You Can Paint Seashore in Watercolour, 2004
You Can Paint Flowers in Watercolour, 2004

Colour reproduction by Colourscan, Singapore
Printed and bound by Printing Express Ltd, Hong Kong

contents

The authors

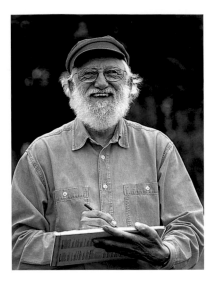

Alwyn Crawshaw

Alwyn Crawshaw has inspired millions of amateur painters and has made seven very popular television series on painting for Channel 4, which have been shown worldwide. He has made many successful videos on painting and is the author of over 20 books on art instruction, all of which are published by HarperCollins. A regular contributor to *Leisure Painter* magazine, Alwyn is Founder of the Society of Amateur Artists, President of the National Acrylic Painters Association, a member of the Society of Equestrian Artists and the British Watercolour Society, a Fellow of the Royal Society of Arts, and an Honorary member of the United Society of Artists. He is listed in the current edition of *Who's Who in Art*, and the Marquis *Who's Who in the World*.

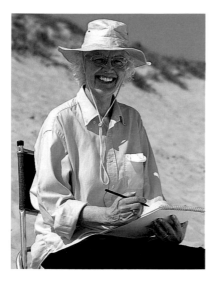 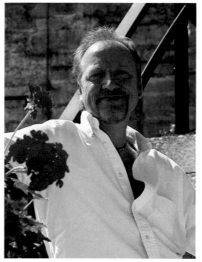

June Crawshaw

June Crawshaw paints in watercolour, acrylic and oil. She is a member of the Society of Women Artists, the British Watercolour Society, the National Acrylic Painters Association and is an Honorary member of the United Society of Artists. She had major joint exhibitions with her husband Alwyn in Tokyo in 1998 and 2001, and in 1992 she helped him to found and launch the Society of Amateur Artists. June writes articles for *Leisure Painter* magazine and has featured in three television series with Alwyn, which have been screened by Channel 4 worldwide. She has her work published as fine art prints and greetings cards. Her first book was published by Collins in 1995. She is listed in the current edition of *Who's Who in Art*.

Trevor Waugh

Trevor Waugh studied at the Slade School of Fine Art in London and is now an established popular painter who runs very successful painting workshops and holidays. In recent years, he has travelled extensively throughout the United States, the Middle East, Morocco, Egypt, France, Italy, Spain and Turkey, painting, running watercolour classes and exhibiting his work. Apart from his original watercolours and oils, Trevor's work is also known to a wide market through his greeting cards, prints and other merchandise. Visit his website at http://www.trevorwaugh.com. His other books, also published by HarperCollins, are *Winning with Watercolour*, which has become a top-selling title, and *You Can Paint Animals in Watercolour*.

materials &

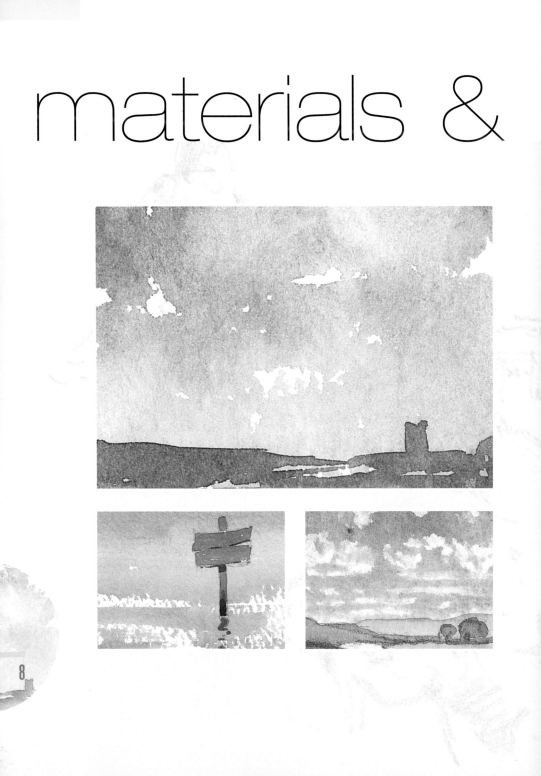

techniques

Before you start painting in watercolour, you will need some basic art materials and a wide range is now available. You can add different brushes, colours and paper as you gain experience. You also need to learn and practise a variety of techniques in order that you may understand how your materials behave and how to create different paint effects.

Basic materials

There is nothing special about the watercolour materials you need for painting. The ones recommended here can be used for any subject, and as a beginner you don't need to buy a whole range of expensive art materials. In fact, the fewer you have, the less you have to learn to use.

Colours

Watercolours come in pans or tubes. Pans are better for beginners as you can control the amount of paint you put on your brush much more easily. There are two qualities of paint: Students' and Artists'. Artists' quality are best but Daler-Rowney Students' Georgian are very good and less expensive. The following colours are ideal for painting landscapes or seascapes: Alizarin Crimson, Yellow Ochre, French Ultramarine, Cadmium Yellow Pale, Cadmium Red, Hooker's Green Dark and, occasionally, Coeruleum blue. For painting flowers, you will need Naples Yellow, Lemon Yellow, Cadmium Yellow, Gamboge, Indian Yellow, Cadmium Orange,

▲ Watercolours come in tubes or pans

Vermilion, Permanent Rose, Permanent Mauve, Phthalo Blue, Cobalt Blue, Phthalo Green, Raw Sienna, Burnt Sienna and a watercolour white.

Brushes

The best watercolour brush to buy is a sable hair brush. These are made from real sable fur, so they are also the most expensive. There are also excellent synthetic brushes on the market that cost much less than sable (for example, Daler-Rowney's Dalon), and some synthetic/sable mix ones. For landscapes and seascapes, use a No.10 for your big brush, a No.6 as your small brush, and a D99 rigger No.2 for thin lines. The higher the number, the larger the brush, and for flowers you will also need No.8, No.14 and No.20 brushes. All round brushes should come to a good tip when wet.

Paper

There are many different makes of paper available, in different weights and textures. In this book, the papers usually used are Bockingford watercolour paper Not surface (this means it does not have a rough surface), and cartridge paper. Both are inexpensive and of excellent quality, and can be bought in different sized pads. Even experienced artists can find it awe-inspiring to sit, brush poised, in front of a large, blank piece of paper. When you are starting out, don't do any paintings larger than 25 x 38 cm (10 x 15 in), although it is not helpful to work in 'miniature' either as you will not get the feel for the movement of the paint and the brush on the paper. And, finally, when watercolour painting you must always have your paper at an angle to allow the paint to run slowly down the page. You can do this by taping it to a sloping drawing board.

▲ Basic equipment for a beginner.

Other equipment

A 2B pencil is good for drawing as it is quite soft but you may also want to use an HB and 4B to give varying degrees of softness in sketching. A putty eraser is useful for rubbing out as it can be used gently without causing too much damage to the paper. A craft knife is essential for sharpening your pencil. You will also need a water container – a jam jar is ideal. Although you will normally mix your colours in the palettes in the lid of your paintbox, you will also need a separate mixing palette or a china plate for larger washes.

MUST KNOW

Practise indoors

Finally, it is a good idea to get used to working with your materials before you venture outside. This will make painting landscapes outdoors much more enjoyable.

Techniques

As a beginner, it is very important to practise some basic techniques with your different materials before you try painting. These will help you to understand how your pencil, paints, brushes and paper behave. There are many ways to create different paint effects, and with practice you will be able to find some different ones of your own.

Using a pencil

Your landscape paintings start with a drawing, so it is important to get used to using a pencil. Also, you will sometimes find that you only have a pencil with you on location, so it is important to feel confident that you can get the most out of just a pencil sketch to make it easy to use when you paint from it at home.

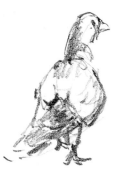

▼ These pencil sketches were done with a 2B pencil. They were drawn to capture an overall image, not small detail.

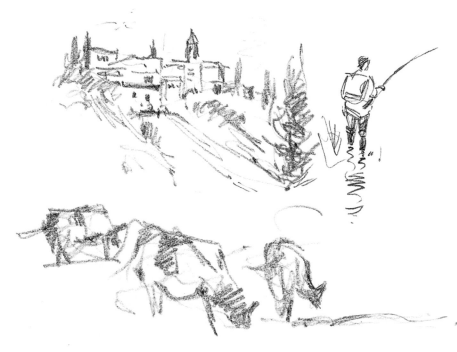

Pencil marks

Using a pencil takes practice, but you will soon get the feel for it. Use ordinary copying paper to practise, as it's inexpensive and you can 'scribble' as much as you like. The most important rule is to sharpen your pencil correctly. The pencil was sharpened to a long point for drawing this page and not sharpened again, and the thin line ovals at the bottom were done last of all!

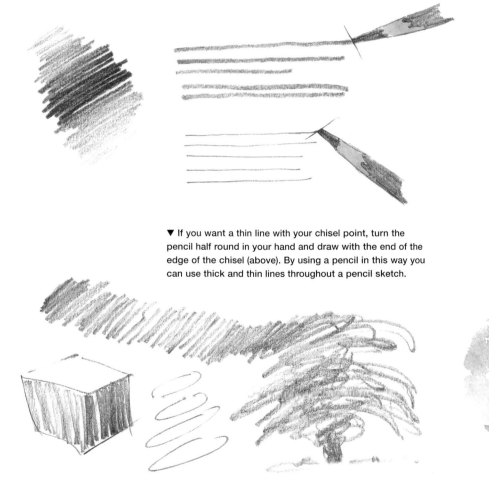

▲ This pencil has a long point. This makes it versatile. As you work, the point wears off and creates a 'chisel point' (below). This allows you to make thick lines for shading.

▼ If you want a thin line with your chisel point, turn the pencil half round in your hand and draw with the end of the edge of the chisel (above). By using a pencil in this way you can use thick and thin lines throughout a pencil sketch.

Brush marks

Use your brushes to produce a variety of different marks. The way you use them gives the painting your own identity, in the same way that when you use a pen for writing it makes your writing individual. With a little practice you will soon find your brush work becoming second nature. Below, a small brush is used for the green strokes, and a rigger for the blue lines.

▶ Paint some thin lines by applying no pressure to the brush. Then try a thicker brush stroke by loading the brush with paint, working up to a drawn line at the top edge and filling in with paint below.

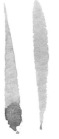

◀ Do two strokes from top to bottom, starting the first without any pressure and then increasing the pressure towards the bottom of the stroke. Start the other with pressure, then gradually ease off.

▲ With plenty of watery paint do a free stroke: this is useful for general 'filling in'.

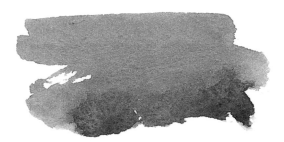

▶ This was painted with very watery paint, which ran to the bottom making puddles. If left to dry these can make an unwanted dark area. Avoid this by soaking the excess paint up with a damp brush before it dries.

▲ Try painting some fine lines using your rigger brush. You will find this brush invaluable for painting thin tree branches and for any other very fine line work.

Dry brush

The 'dry brush' technique is used in almost every watercolour. As a natural brush stroke starts to run out of paint, the paint hits and misses the paper and leaves flecks unpainted. This effect can be achieved where you want it either by using less paint in your brush or by pushing the brush hairs down at the ferrule end (the metal end that holds the hairs) while you paint.

▲ The rougher the paper surface, the more exaggerated the dry brush effect.

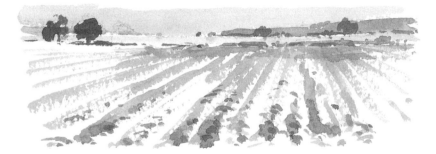

▲ A ploughed field painted using this technique.

▲ The dry brush effect is the ideal technique for showing sparkling sunlit water.

Washes

If you are now familiar with your brushes, the next stage is to practise making some washes. The wash is the most fundamental technique in watercolour painting. Remember always to keep your paper at an angle to allow the paint to run downwards naturally.

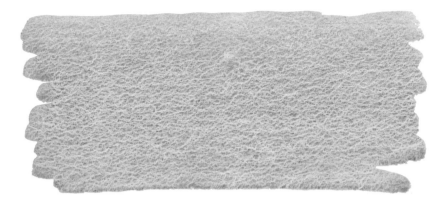

▲ Flat wash

Load a brush with plenty of watery paint, and make a definite stroke across the top of the paper. Lift the brush off, fill with paint and take the next stroke across, letting it run and mix with the one above. Continue this.

▲ Graded wash

Paint this in the same way as the flat wash but as you work down add water to the paint in the palette to dilute the colour and repeat this with each brush stroke.

▲ Colour graded wash

Work the same way as the graded wash, but instead of water add different colours into your palette as you work down. This is a great way to paint a sunset.

Wet-on-wet

This is an exciting technique; when a wet colour is put on top of another wet colour the colours merge and mix in their own way. This creates 'happy accidents': areas where you did not control the results, but which look great. With experience you will learn to create and control happy accidents.

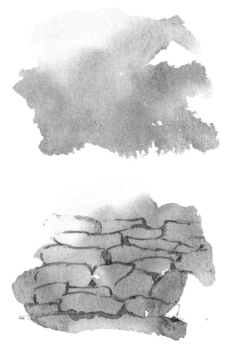

▲ Paint yellow, red and blue wet-on-wet, letting the colours mix and merge. When dry, use darker paint and your small brush to paint some lines to represent a stone wall.

▲ Use the same colour mix as before, but with blue as your main colour. When dry, suggest the simple silhouette of hills and a church. Wet-on-wet is great for painting skies.

Wet-on-dry

When you paint wet paint onto dry paint you will always get a hard edge. The paint must be totally dry, or the wet paint will merge into the damp colour to give a blurred edge.

Soft edges

Soft edges are as important as hard edges and you will use this technique throughout a painting. A soft edge can be achieved in several different ways.

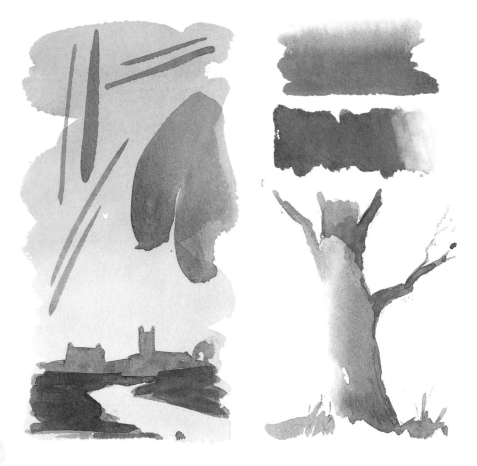

▲ Paint a colour wash and let it dry. Then paint shapes and brush strokes over it. To paint thin lines use less water in your brush, or the paint will spread.

▲ Start painting with water first and then add colour. Or add water at the end of an area of colour. Also try lifting out for a soft edge (see opposite), as for the tree trunk here.

Lifting out

Lifting out is when an area of paint is removed. This technique can be used to correct mistakes, or deliberately to lighten a darker area of the painting. Some papers lift out better than others, and there will usually be a slight stain left on the paper, depending on the colour of the paint. You can lift out using tissue or a brush.

▲ Paint an area of blue and while it is still very wet press a screwed-up soft tissue onto it, lifting off the paint to represent clouds. A simple technique, but very impressive.

▲ A brush gives more control over the area to be lifted out. Let the paint dry then brush water over the area and blot with tissue. You may have to repeat this a few times.

Easy colour mixing

When you look at a painting you see hundreds of different colours. However, don't worry; these can be simplified. For example, the predominant landscape colours are blues (in the sky), greens (fields and trees) and browns (earth colours). All colours can be mixed using just three primary colours: red, yellow and blue. Different shades of red, yellow and blue mix to give a wide range of different colours.

Starter palette

Begin with the colours below in your starter palette. Yellow Ochre, Alizarin Crimson and French Ultramarine are useful primary colours as are Cadmium Yellow Pale, Cadmium Red and Coeruleum. For landscapes, one 'mixed' colour, Hooker's Green Dark, is useful as different primary colours may be added to it to make different greens. To make colours lighter you add water, and to make them darker add less water or more paint (pigment).

Basic starter palette

| Yellow Ochre | Alizarin Crimson | French Ultramarine | Cadmium Yellow Pale | Cadmium Red | Coeruleum | Hooker's Green Dark |

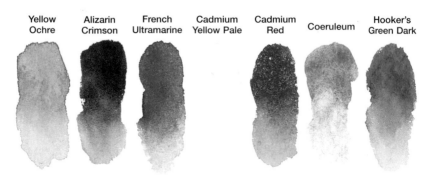

MUST KNOW

The golden rule

The most important rule to remember when mixing colours is to put the predominant colour into your palette first (with water), and then add the other colours to it, usually in smaller amounts. For example, if you wanted to mix a yellowy green, you would put yellow into your palette and then add smaller amounts of blue until you reach your desired colour.

Practise colour mixing

Below left are two examples of mixing greens, one a yellowy green, the other a dark blue-green, showing how the predominant colour is used first. Below right two different sets of primary colours have been mixed to show the range of colours you can get by mixing different yellows, reds and blues. With practice, you will be amazed at what you can achieve with colour mixing: you will find it easier than you expect and it is very enjoyable.

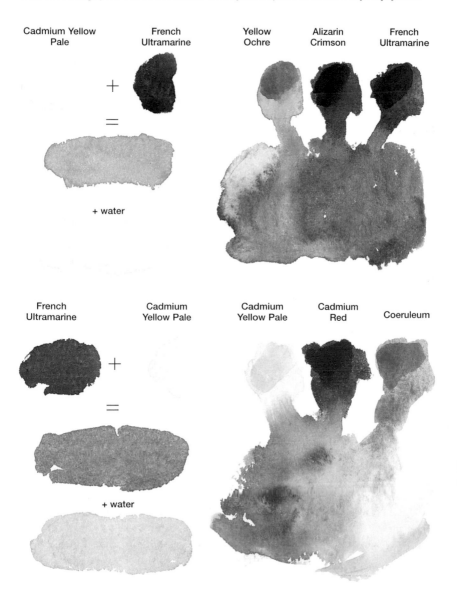

Cadmium Yellow Pale

French Ultramarine

+ water

Yellow Ochre

Alizarin Crimson

French Ultramarine

French Ultramarine

Cadmium Yellow Pale

+ water

Cadmium Yellow Pale

Cadmium Red

Coeruleum

Mixing landscape greens

Here are some of the different greens that can be mixed from your starter palette. Add the second colour gradually to make the mixed colour darker.

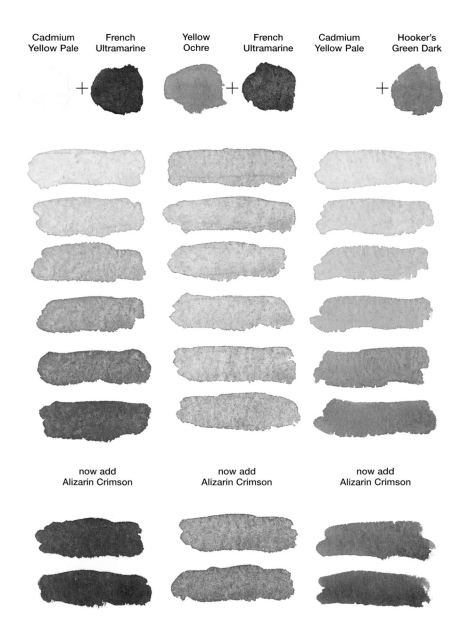

Cadmium
Yellow Pale   French
                 Ultramarine   Yellow
                                  Ochre   French
                                             Ultramarine   Cadmium
                                                              Yellow Pale   Hooker's
                                                                               Green Dark

now add
Alizarin Crimson   now add
                      Alizarin Crimson   now add
                                            Alizarin Crimson

Mixing landscape browns

Like the greens, you can mix a wide variety of browns from just a few colours. Add the second colour gradually to make the mixed colour darker.

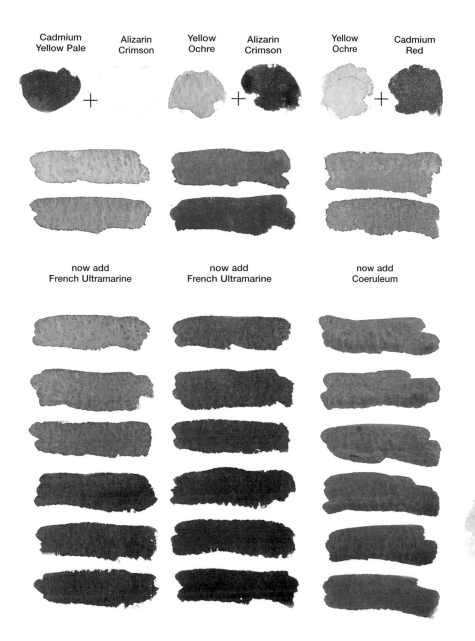

Cadmium Yellow Pale   Alizarin Crimson   Yellow Ochre   Alizarin Crimson   Yellow Ochre   Cadmium Red

now add French Ultramarine   now add French Ultramarine   now add Coeruleum

Making objects look 3-d

The only way in which you can make an object appear real and three-dimensional, not just flat, is to add shadows. Look at the boxes below and the objects on the opposite page. They become real objects only by adding shadows to the flat shapes. Light against dark will always show shape and form and make objects look three-dimensional.

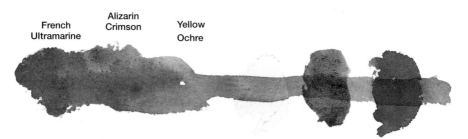

French
Ultramarine

Alizarin
Crimson

Yellow
Ochre

▲ Mix French Ultramarine, Alizarin Crimson and a little Yellow Ochre for a general shadow colour. Because watercolour is transparent, when you paint this shadow colour over a dry colour, the colour will show through, but will appear darker, giving the illusion of a shadow.

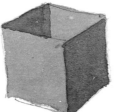

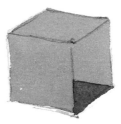

▲ This flat shape is meaningless until a shadow is added to give it shape and form, then it becomes an open box. The box lying on its side comes from the same flat shape, but the shadow is in a different place.

◀ Here the same flat shape has a roof. The cast shadow from the box makes it appear to be resting on the ground.

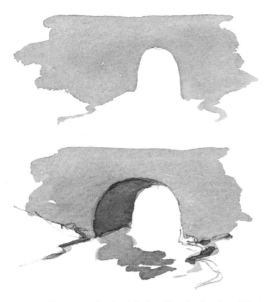

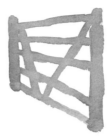

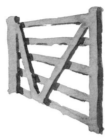

▲ This bridge looks flat (top) before the shadow is painted as shown above.

▲ With only a few dark shadow lines, the gate looks three-dimensional.

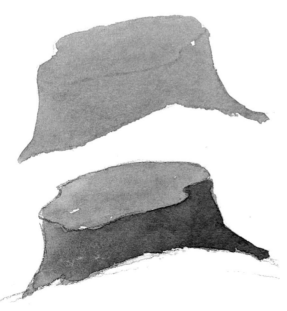

▲ Notice how the shadow on the tree stump has been given a soft edge to make it appear rounded. Remember to wait until the first wash is dry before you start painting any hard-edge shadows.

want to know more?

Take it to the next level...

Go to...
► **Techniques** – page 80
► **Using your brush** – page 128
► **Using colour** – page 136

Other sources
► **Art shops**
  try different materials
► **Art classes**
  many colleges offer painting courses
► **Videos**
  painting videos from Teaching Art and APV Films
► **Specialist magazines**
  The Artist, *Leisure Painter* and *Artists & Illustrators*
► **Publications**
  visit www.collins.co.uk for Collins art books

painting

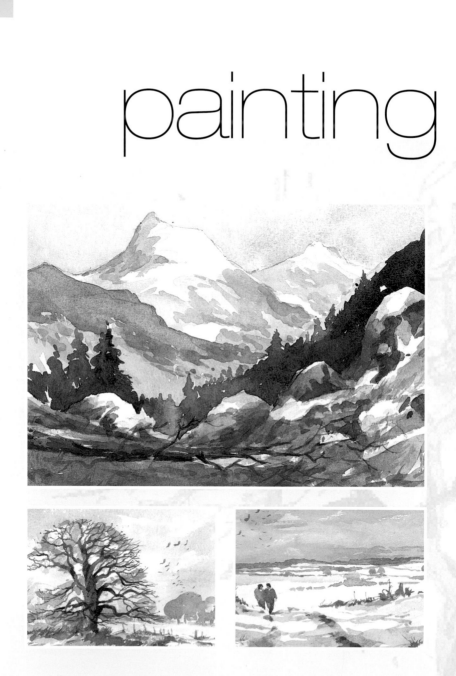

landscapes

Landscape is everywhere you look and it is perhaps the most popular subject for artists. For a beginner, just looking at a view of a complex landscape can be daunting, but remember the old adage, 'don't run before you can walk'. By following the expert advice in this section, you will soon progress and will be painting good landscapes sooner than you think.

Skies

I believe the sky is the most important part of a landscape painting because it sets the mood. If you reflect the mood of the sky in the rest of your painting, you will have given the whole painting atmosphere. When practising skies, adding land, however simple, will help to give scale to the sky.

Heavy sky

Notice how clouds get smaller and narrower as they go to the horizon. This gives the illusion of distance. Remember the 'happy accidents' you get when working wet-on-wet. Skies with clouds are full of them!

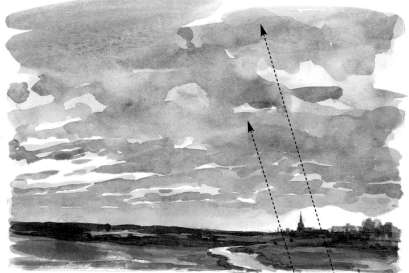

▲ I painted the whole of the sky and into the landscape in one wash, wet-on-wet, changing the colours as I worked. When this was dry I painted a darker wash to give more shape to the clouds, using water to soften the cloud edges and let some colours merge. I then painted in the landscape, keeping it simple, reflecting the mood of the sky in the colours.

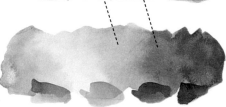

Hooker's Green Dark + Yellow Ochre
+ Alizarin Crimson + French Ultramarine

Skies in pencil

Copy skies from life, using a 2B pencil to start with. You are not concerned about colour, so all your concentration can be on the formation of clouds and their different tones. Even white clouds have shape and form, and shades of dark against light.

▶ Practise using your pencil flat to get a very broad shading line. This will help you to draw and shade the clouds more quickly – sometimes they can move fast!

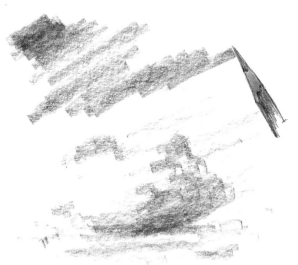

▲ This cloud formation was moving slowly and therefore speed was not of the essence. I shaded the 'blue' sky dark, to help create a contrast with the clouds.

▲ These clouds were moving fast, but I was after the general impression, not each individual cloud shape. Note how they get smaller to the horizon.

One-wash sky

This is a very simple sky painted with only one wash, wet-on-wet. I used my large brush for the sky and the very simple landscape. Notice how the dark shadow of the clouds has run into the blue sky and given the impression of a rain shower. This was a controlled 'happy accident'.

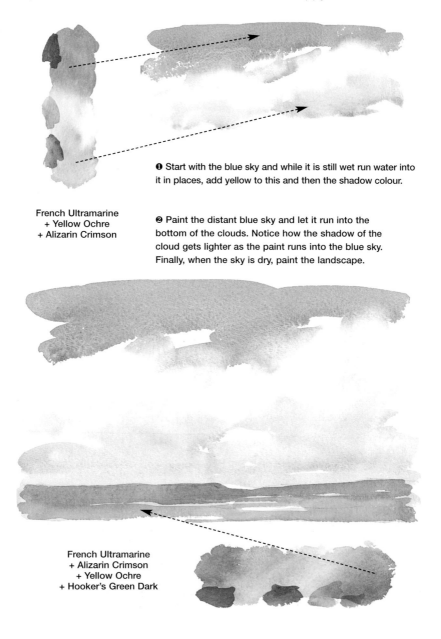

❶ Start with the blue sky and while it is still wet run water into it in places, add yellow to this and then the shadow colour.

French Ultramarine
+ Yellow Ochre
+ Alizarin Crimson

❷ Paint the distant blue sky and let it run into the bottom of the clouds. Notice how the shadow of the cloud gets lighter as the paint runs into the blue sky. Finally, when the sky is dry, paint the landscape.

French Ultramarine
+ Alizarin Crimson
+ Yellow Ochre
+ Hooker's Green Dark

Sunset

You must be careful when you paint a very colourful sunset. Sunsets look fantastic in real life and very inspiring, but as a painting they can look 'over the top' and too colourful. Therefore, until you have gained experience in painting with watercolour, tone down the colours.

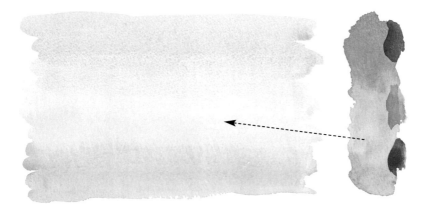

❶ Using your big brush, paint a graded colour wash down from the sky into the landscape.

French Ultramarine
+ Yellow Ochre
+ Alizarin Crimson

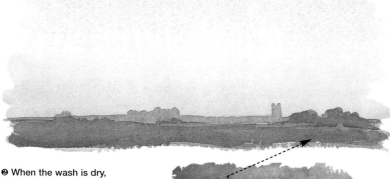

❷ When the wash is dry, paint in the landscape. The warm colours of the underpainting (the sky) help to give the ground colours an evening atmosphere.

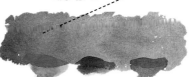

Yellow Ochre + Alizarin Crimson
+ French Ultramarine

Stormy sky

This stormy sky looks very complicated, but it is painted in the same way as the other skies, wet-on-wet, just using stronger colours. There are 'happy accidents', both controlled and uncontrolled. Painting wet-on-wet means that your painting will not look exactly the same as this.

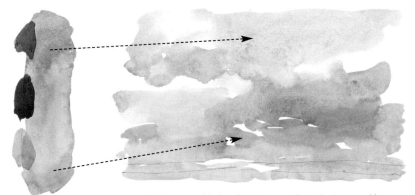

French Ultramarine
+ Alizarin Crimson
+ Yellow Ochre

❶ Using your big brush, start a wash at the top, working down the sky, changing your colours as you paint. Keep the paint watery so the colours can merge together. Paint into the landscape and let it dry.

❷ Add darker colours for the heavy clouds. Then paint the landscape. Using only water, gently brush out the sky and landscape under the 'black' cloud to give the illusion of rain.

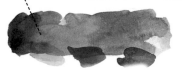

Yellow Ochre + Alizarin Crimson
+ French Ultramarine

Sunny day

For this sky I used the lifting-out technique shown on page 19 to indicate the clouds. The impression of a sunny day was helped by adding shadows on the landscape, which are being cast from the clouds onto the grass.

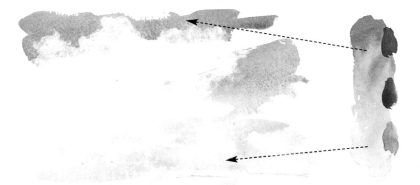

❶ Paint the blue sky first, leaving some white unpainted paper, then change the colours as you paint down to the landscape. Blot out the clouds with screwed-up tissue.

French Ultramarine
+ Alizarin Crimson
+ Yellow Ochre

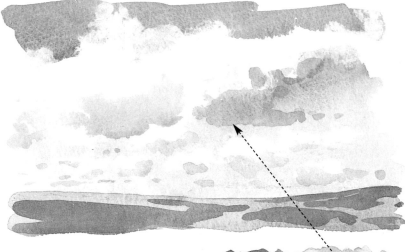

❷ When dry, paint in the yellow for the sunlit clouds and paint shadows on the clouds. Finally, paint the ground and the shadows being cast by the clouds.

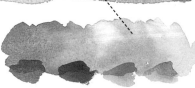

French Ultramarine + Alizarin Crimson
+ Yellow Ochre + Hooker's Green Dark

EXERCISE **Paint a sky**

In this exercise the clouds are painted with one wash using the wet-on-wet technique. The crisp hard edges are created by leaving white paper. Painting wet-on-wet means that your finished painting will look different from mine: use my painting as a guide.

The palette

French Ultramarine   Alizarin Crimson   Yellow Ochre   Hooker's Green Dark

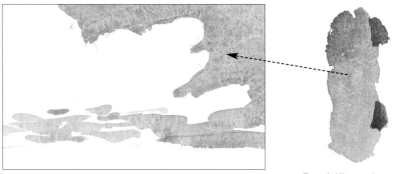

French Ultramarine + Alizarin Crimson

❶ Draw the clouds in with a 2B pencil and paint the blue sky. As you paint under the large clouds make your brush strokes horizontal.

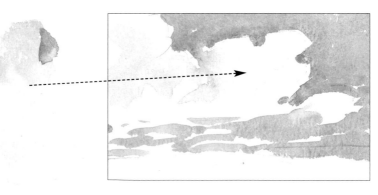

Yellow Ochre

❷ Now paint the yellow sunlit areas of the clouds, letting the yellow touch the blue sky in places.

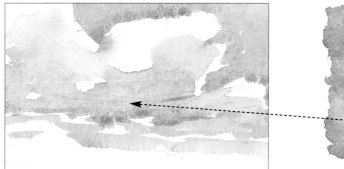

❸ While the yellow is still wet, paint the shadows onto the clouds (wet-on-wet).

French Ultramarine
+ Alizarin Crimson
+ Yellow Ochre

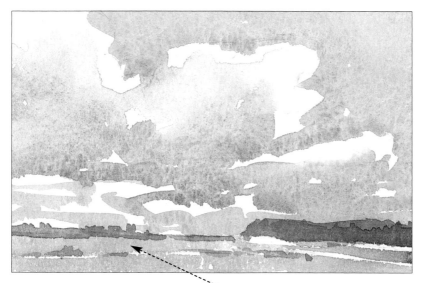

❹ Paint in the land. Notice how the white unpainted paper stands out after the land is painted. This makes the sunlit areas sparkle.

Hooker's Green Dark + Yellow Ochre
+ Alizarin Crimson + French Ultramarine

Trees

Most landscapes would be uninteresting without trees. Like
the sky, they have an important role in your paintings. No
matter how simple the sky and background, if the trees look
plausible, the painting will be good. Some trees (fir, poplar
and cypress) are easy to paint; others, like a large oak, are
not, but if you practise, your confidence and ability will grow.

Hedgerow trees

Look at the simple background to this tree painting. The distant trees on
the right are just silhouettes and the sky is a simple wash. But because the
trees in the foreground have more detail, they stand out from the
background, giving space to the landscape.

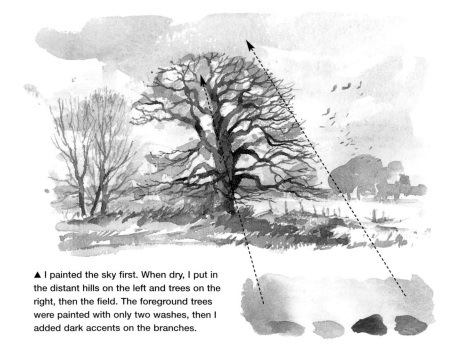

▲ I painted the sky first. When dry, I put in
the distant hills on the left and trees on the
right, then the field. The foreground trees
were painted with only two washes, then I
added dark accents on the branches.

Hooker's Green Dark + Yellow Ochre
+ Alizarin Crimson + French Ultramarine

Winter tree in watercolour

When you paint the branches on a tree, always paint the brush strokes in the direction the tree is growing. Don't attempt to draw in the very small, feathery branches as these are usually worked with a wash or dry brush.

❶ Draw in with your 2B pencil and, using your small brush, start to paint up the trunk.

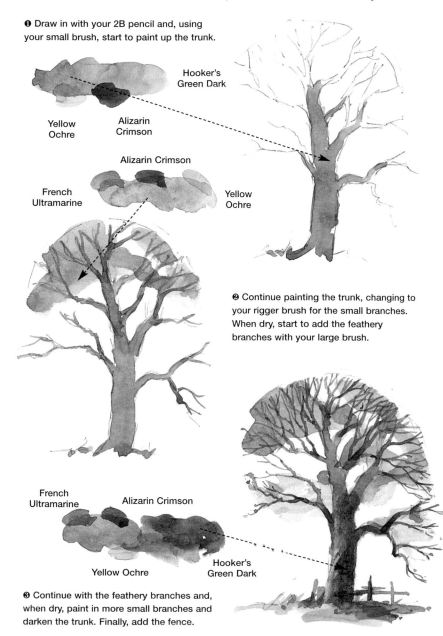

Hooker's Green Dark

Yellow Ochre

Alizarin Crimson

Alizarin Crimson

French Ultramarine

Yellow Ochre

❷ Continue painting the trunk, changing to your rigger brush for the small branches. When dry, start to add the feathery branches with your large brush.

French Ultramarine

Alizarin Crimson

Yellow Ochre

Hooker's Green Dark

❸ Continue with the feathery branches and, when dry, paint in more small branches and darken the trunk. Finally, add the fence.

Summer tree in watercolour

When you are painting from life, be aware of the scale of the tree. Painting a tree the size I have on this page, an individual leaf would be smaller than a full stop, so any 'blobs' that you paint are not individual leaves, but bunches of leaves.

❶ Draw the tree with your 2B pencil. Start painting by working up the trunk, using your small brush.

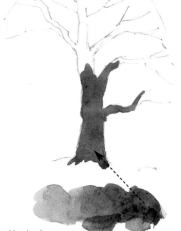

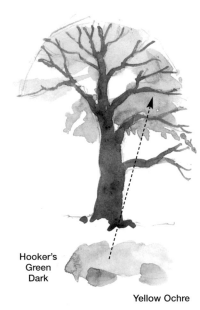

Hooker's
Green
Dark

Yellow Ochre

Hooker's
Green Dark

Alizarin
Crimson

French
Ultramarine

❷ Continue and paint in the smaller branches. When this is dry, start at the top and paint the foliage over the branches.

❸ Continue with the foliage. When dry, paint the darker areas. Notice how the trunk is lifted out in the middle of the tree to let the foliage take its place. This helps the tree to look more 3-D. Don't forget the fence – it gives scale!

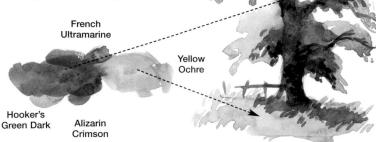

French
Ultramarine

Yellow
Ochre

Hooker's
Green Dark

Alizarin
Crimson

Autumn tree in watercolour

Nothing beats the autumn colouring of deciduous trees. But, like a sunset, autumnal colours can look over the top in a painting, so be careful. Usually there are some green leaves left on some trees, helping to avoid too many bright colours, and you can add evergreen trees to your painting.

Yellow Ochre

Alizarin Crimson

❶ Draw the tree with your 2B pencil. Then paint it using your small brush.

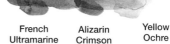

French Ultramarine   Alizarin Crimson   Yellow Ochre

❷ Start at the top and add the darker foliage colours and continue down the trunk.

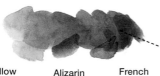

Yellow Ochre   Alizarin Crimson   French Ultramarine

❸ Finish painting in the dark foliage colour and then paint the trunk and branches darker. Add some new darker branches at the bottom, some shadows and the fence.

Sketching trees

If you are a little nervous of going out to sketch from life, then copy the sketches on these pages first. They will give you the confidence to sit and sketch outdoors. I have painted them very simply, using simple brush stroke washes and adding some details with a rigger brush.

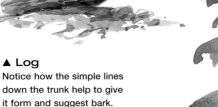

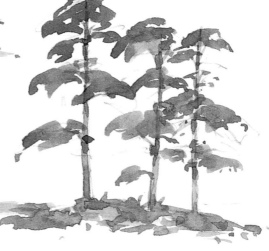

▲ Log
Notice how the simple lines down the trunk help to give it form and suggest bark.

▶ Fir trees
The foliage was painted in one go, using horizontal free brush strokes.

▼ Apple tree
It was important to observe and draw the branches, showing sunlight and shadows.

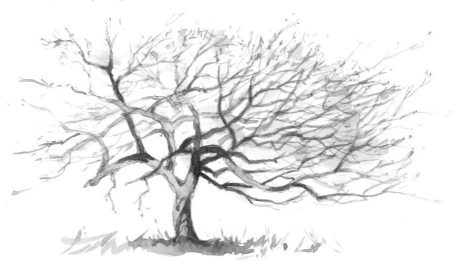

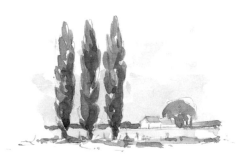

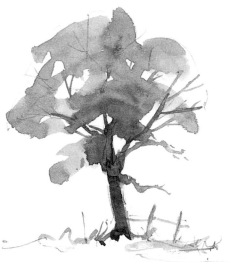

▲ Poplar trees

Like the fir trees, simple brush strokes were used, but this time painted downwards.

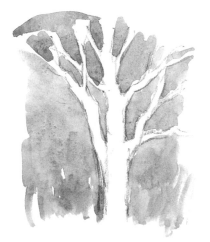

▲ Summer tree

Use the same brush strokes as the fir trees, but make them bolder and let them run together in places.

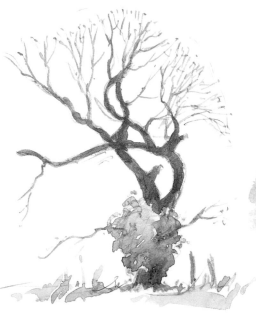

▲ 'Light against dark' tree

It is sometimes necessary to show a tree light against dark, effectively 'reversed out'. This technique needs practice.

▶ Winter tree

This looks more complicated because of the small thin branches. These are done with a rigger brush, just as if I were drawing with a pencil, but the paint must be watery for it to flow easily.

EXERCISE **Paint autumn trees**

Paint these two trees the same way that you have been practising on the previous pages. Perhaps the autumn-coloured one should have lost its leaves by now, but with the green grass and the dark tree it makes a pleasant painting. Don't forget that you can use your artistic licence!

The palette

| Hooker's Green Dark | Alizarin Crimson | French Ultramarine | Yellow Ochre |

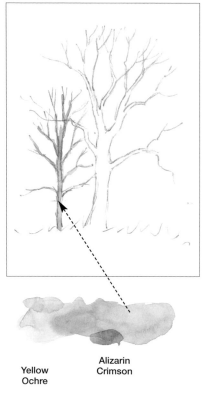 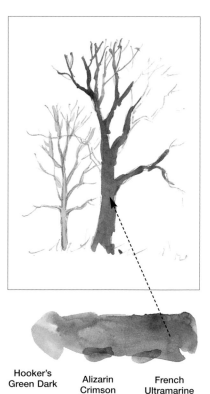

Yellow Ochre — Alizarin Crimson

Hooker's Green Dark — Alizarin Crimson — French Ultramarine

❶ Draw the trees with a 2B pencil and paint in the trunk and branches of the autumn-coloured one using your rigger.

❷ Using the same brush, paint the large tree, working the trunk upwards, then adding the thin branches.

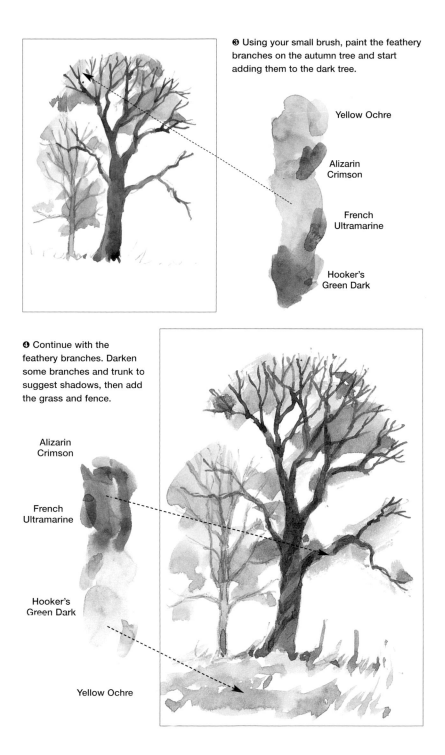

❸ Using your small brush, paint the feathery branches on the autumn tree and start adding them to the dark tree.

Yellow Ochre

Alizarin
Crimson

French
Ultramarine

Hooker's
Green Dark

❹ Continue with the feathery branches. Darken some branches and trunk to suggest shadows, then add the grass and fence.

Alizarin
Crimson

French
Ultramarine

Hooker's
Green Dark

Yellow Ochre

Creating distance

Follow nature's rules to create the illusion of distance in a painting. Firstly, everything gets smaller as it gets further away. Secondly, you see more detail the nearer the object is to you. Thirdly, cool or cold colours (blues) recede into the distance, while warm colours (reds) advance. Fourthly, perspective or directional lines help to give the impression of distance. Finally, making objects 'misty' or paler helps to imply distance.

Distant landscape

Study the painting below and you can see these 'rules' being applied. Next time you are in the countryside check them against what you see. It will surprise you, for instance, how green a close-up field is compared to a field or hills in the distance, which appear blue-green or even just blue. In a painting we can exaggerate these rules to make distance more obvious.

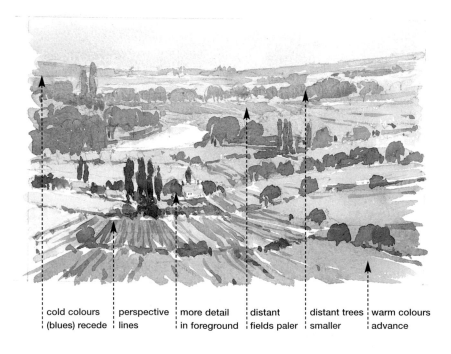

cold colours (blues) recede | perspective lines | more detail in foreground | distant fields paler | distant trees smaller | warm colours advance

Distant hills

This simplified example shows how cool colours (blues) recede and give the illusion of distance. It also shows how colours get paler the further away they are. Notice how I have put a warm-coloured field in the foreground.

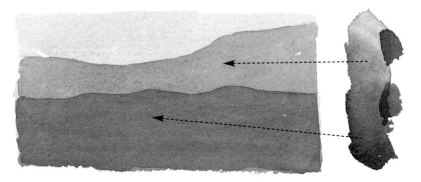

❶ Paint a pale blue wash down to the field. When dry, paint over the distant and nearer hills with a slightly darker wash. Then paint an even darker blue wash over the last one to show the nearer hills.

French Ultramarine
+ Alizarin Crimson

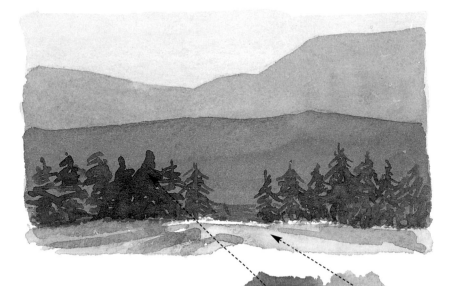

❷ Now paint the dark trees and, finally, the field. Notice the brush strokes are painted in perspective. These are simple techniques but they all help to give the illusion of distance.

French Ultramarine + Alizarin Crimson
+ Yellow Ochre

Misty landscape

This is a very easy way to show distance in a painting. Paler colours in the distance help, but here we are letting one of nature's weather conditions assist too – mist. I have also added a path, which leads you into the picture and takes your eye away into the distance.

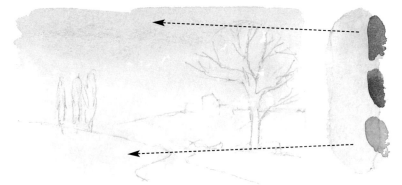

❶ First draw in with a 2B pencil. Paint a graded colour wash over the whole painting. Leave the path unpainted.

French Ultramarine
+ Alizarin Crimson
+ Yellow Ochre

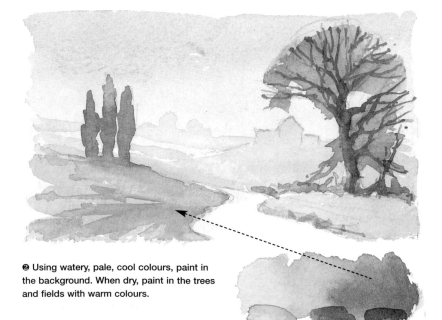

❷ Using watery, pale, cool colours, paint in the background. When dry, paint in the trees and fields with warm colours.

Yellow Ochre + Alizarin Crimson
+ French Ultramarine

Distant village

Although this painting includes bright-coloured sunny fields, the feeling of distance has still been achieved. The distant hills are dark blue, the silhouette of the church paler blue. The clouds all get smaller to the horizon. Finally, the road leads your eye towards the distant village.

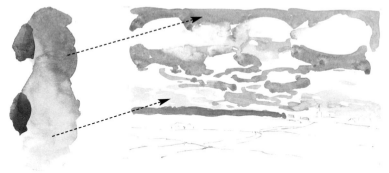

French Ultramarine + Alizarin Crimson

❶ Make a sketch with a 2B pencil. Paint the sky, leaving unpainted areas for clouds and making them progressively smaller down to the horizon. Paint in the background hills.

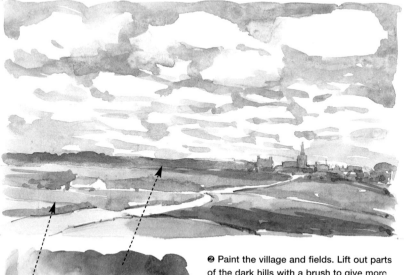

❷ Paint the village and fields. Lift out parts of the dark hills with a brush to give more distant atmosphere. Paint a pale shadow on the road and darker ones on the fields.

Hooker's Green Dark + Yellow Ochre + Alizarin Crimson + French Ultramarine

Foreground path

In a painting you can help the foreground to look close by the way you paint the distance. In this picture the blue trees in the distance help the warmer coloured foreground to look closer. Always remember that cold colours will make objects recede, warm colours advance.

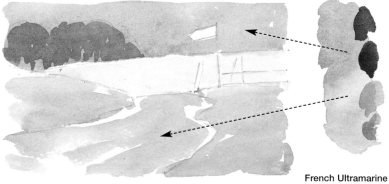

❶ Paint a wash for the sky, then the green fields and path. When dry, paint in the distant trees.

French Ultramarine
+ Alizarin Crimson
+ Yellow Ochre
+ Hooker's Green Dark

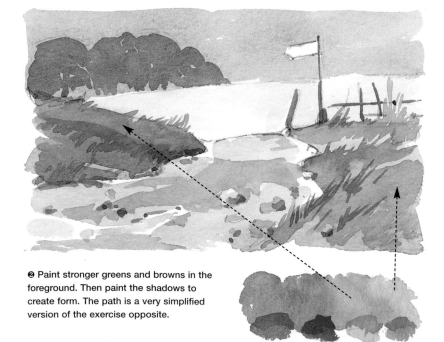

❷ Paint stronger greens and browns in the foreground. Then paint the shadows to create form. The path is a very simplified version of the exercise opposite.

French Ultramarine + Alizarin Crimson
+ Yellow Ochre + Hooker's Green Dark

Cart track

The directional line running from the long grass leads you to the distant trees, which give scale to the painting and to the foreground. The long grass gives scale to the clumps of earth and stones. As when you paint trees, your foreground should include something to show scale.

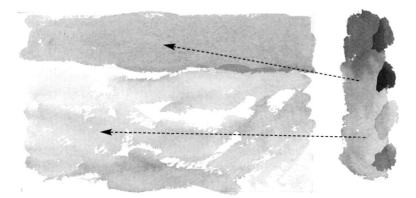

❶ Paint the sky with a wash. Using wet-on-wet and dry brush techniques, paint in the underpainting. It is important to paint the brush strokes in the direction of the contours of the land.

French Ultramarine
+ Alizarin Crimson
+ Yellow Ochre
+ Hooker's Green Dark

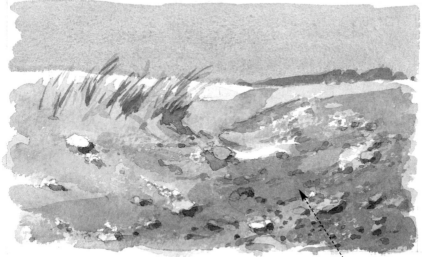

❷ Paint darker areas to give form to the land, leaving lighter areas showing. Paint the shadows to create clumps of earth and stones. Define some stones with a 2B pencil.

Yellow Ochre + Hooker's Green Dark
+ French Ultramarine + Alizarin Crimson

Water

The biggest mistake beginners make when they start to paint water is to overpaint it. The more you overpaint, the less realistic it becomes. The key is to keep it simple. Once you can paint realistic water, no matter how simple, people will stop and look twice at your painting, so it is worth practising.

The old windmill

Here the water reflects the sky colour. The dark reflection of the windmill contrasts with the white reflection of the sail. Paint reflections with the same movement as the water. If the water is still, the reflection will be mirror-like. If the water has movement, the reflections will be broken by the movement.

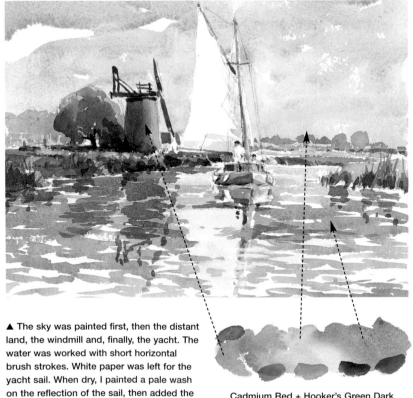

▲ The sky was painted first, then the distant land, the windmill and, finally, the yacht. The water was worked with short horizontal brush strokes. White paper was left for the yacht sail. When dry, I painted a pale wash on the reflection of the sail, then added the dark reflections. The shadow on the windmill was painted with a soft edge.

Cadmium Red + Hooker's Green Dark
+ Yellow Ochre + Alizarin Crimson
+ French Ultramarine

Reflections

One of the most convincing ways to paint water is to show a reflection. If for any reason there isn't a reflection on the water you are painting, or the reflection is very small, then put one in or exaggerate the small one. Use your artistic licence. But above all, keep it simple.

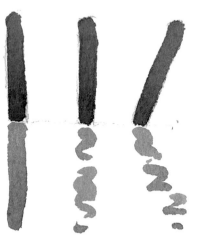

▲ Look at these three posts. The first one has a reflection in still water. The second is reflected in moving water. The third is also in moving water; note how the reflection is at the opposite angle to the post. The water is left as unpainted paper: there is no other visual reference to water and yet the reflections make it look like water.

MUST KNOW

Reflections

As a general rule, remember that all pale objects reflect a little darker than the object, and dark objects reflect a little lighter.

▲ Keep your water and reflections simple. These are very simple but they work

Moving water

Moving water in a river, or where it has been disturbed by the wind or boat traffic, is extremely easy to create in watercolour and will always look impressive. Notice how the light catches the top of the ripples of water and thereby creates the feeling of movement.

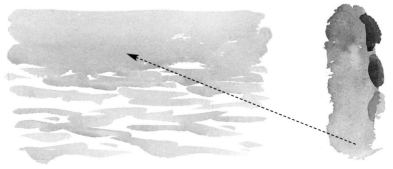

❶ Paint a wash from the top, then continue using broken horizontal brush strokes, leaving white paper for the reflected areas of light.

French Ultramarine
+ Alizarin Crimson
+ Yellow Ochre

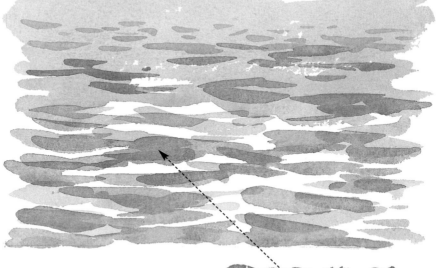

❷ When this is dry, start at the top with darker paint and the same brush strokes, making them larger as you work down. It is important still to leave some unpainted paper to show reflected light.

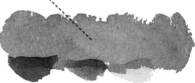

French Ultramarine + Alizarin Crimson
+ Yellow Ochre

Estuary

This is a perfect example of how water painted very, very simply can be very effective. I left the water as white paper until I had painted the surrounding land areas. Then I painted various subtle colours on the areas of white paper, added some reflections, and the water was finished.

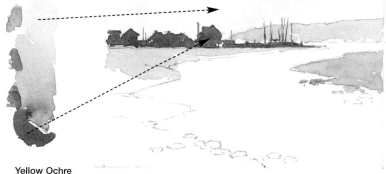

Yellow Ochre
+ Alizarin Crimson
+ French Ultramarine

❶ Paint the sky to the start of the mud flats. When dry, paint the silhouette of the headland and the buildings.

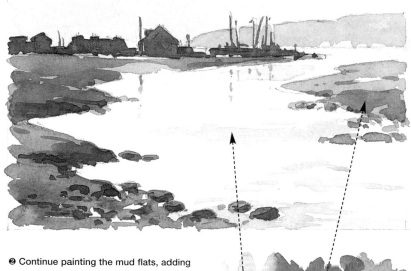

❷ Continue painting the mud flats, adding some darker areas and shadows to show form. Paint the water with different colours using horizontal brush strokes. The river looks bright as it is light against dark.

French Ultramarine + Hooker's Green Dark
+ Alizarin Crimson + Yellow Ochre

EXERCISE Paint reflections

This exercise shows some typical reflections in moving water. When painting moving water from nature, reflections can be difficult to define. Half close your eyes, concentrate just on the reflections, and you will begin to see their general shapes. Don't let your eyes move with the flow of the water.

The palette

| French Ultramarine | Alizarin Crimson | Yellow Ochre | Hooker's Green Dark |

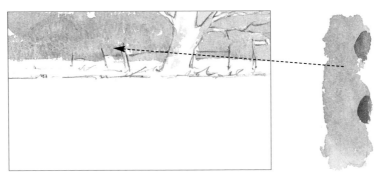

❶ Draw the tree and fence with your 2B pencil. Now paint in the sky, using your large brush.

French Ultramarine
+ Alizarin Crimson

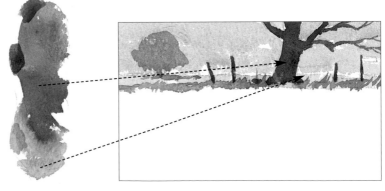

Hooker's Green Dark
+ Alizarin Crimson
+ Yellow Ochre

❷ Paint in the grass and the distant tree. Now paint the fence and large tree, and add the shadows.

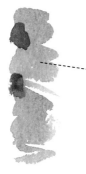

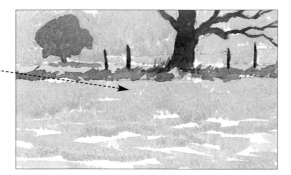

French Ultramarine
+ Alizarin Crimson

❸ Paint the water, starting with a wash and changing into broken horizontal brush strokes.

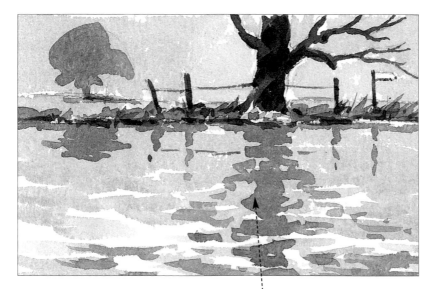

❹ Paint the reflections all the same colour. Let them become more 'disturbed' as you paint down the water to show the water movement.

Yellow Ochre + Alizarin Crimson
+ French Ultramarine

Snow

Creating the illusion of snow in a watercolour landscape is very similar to painting water. You leave plenty of unpainted paper for the lightest snow, and use shadows to define the snow in the same way you use reflections to help create the effect of water. It is important to remember that a shadow falling on snow can be as dark as it would be on a normal landscape.

Late afternoon snow

Here I used warm colours in the distance to suggest the end of the day, and left white paper to show the snow in the foreground. The shadows help to create the contours of the ground. The two people, painted in last, give scale to the painting. Look how simply I painted the distant fields, and notice how they get smaller to the horizon. This creates the impression of distance.

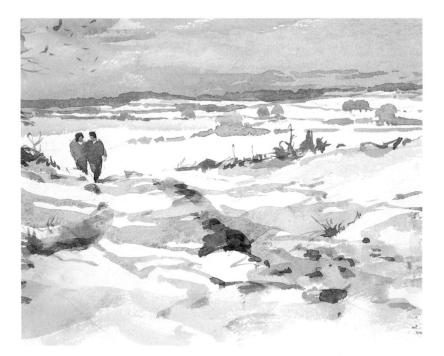

▲ I painted the sky first down to the horizon with my large brush, then the distant hedges to suggest the fields using my small brush. The snow shadows were painted with my large brush and foreground details with my small brush.

Thick snow

If you look at the first stage in this exercise, you can see how leaving just white paper for snow works well. However, notice also how it is flat with no form. You need to add shadows to define it.

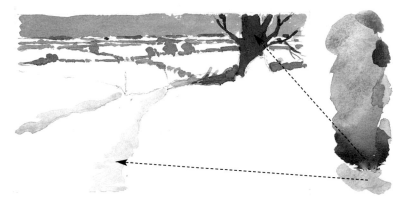

❶ Draw in with your 2B pencil. Paint the sky and distant trees, then the large tree and hedge, leaving white paper at the bottom of the trunk to represent snow. Paint in the two shadows to show the track.

Coeruleum
+ Alizarin Crimson
+ Yellow Ochre
+ Hooker's Green Dark

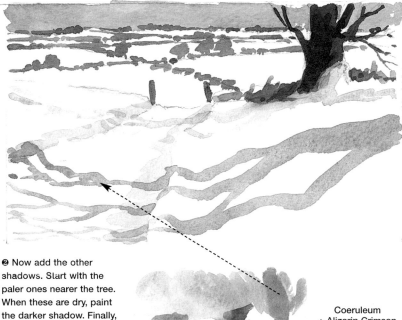

❷ Now add the other shadows. Start with the paler ones nearer the tree. When these are dry, paint the darker shadow. Finally, put in the gateposts to give an impression of scale.

Coeruleum
+ Alizarin Crimson

Mountains

Not all of us have the chance to paint mountains from life. If you do visit a mountainous area on holiday, make sure you take plenty of photographs when you are out sketching to use as reference once you are back at home. On certain days you have to work quickly as a mountain can disappear behind mist or clouds within minutes, and remain hidden for hours.

Sunlit valley

This shows how the mountains are painted paler than the foreground, helping to give the illusion of distance. The farthest mountain is painted smaller, adding to this effect (see page 48). The fir trees are only silhouettes but, with the foreground boulders and fallen tree, they give the picture scale.

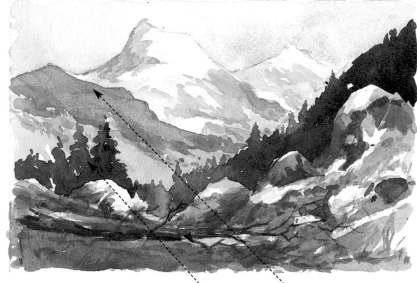

▲ I painted the sky first, leaving the mountain shapes as white paper, followed by the shadows on the mountains and the green sunlit areas. When this was dry, the fir trees were added and finally the foreground boulders, the fallen tree and the shadows.

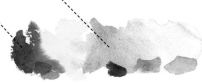

Hooker's Green Dark
+ Cadmium Yellow Pale + Alizarin Crimson
+ Coeruleum + Yellow Ochre

PAINTING LANDSCAPES

Mountains in summer

Mountains without snow sometimes look a little sombre and uninteresting. However, if you catch them with the sun on them they will change dramatically. When you are outdoors sketching, you often have to wait for the sun to hit your mountain, but it's worth the wait.

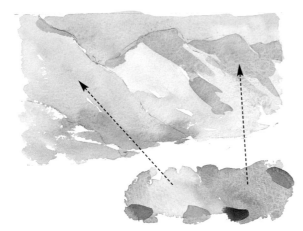

❶ Paint in the sky and go over the distant mountains. When dry, paint a darker shadow on the farthest mountain, then continue painting the others. Let your brush strokes follow their downward slopes.

Hooker's Green Dark
+ Yellow Ochre
+ Alizarin Crimson
+ French Ultramarine

❷ Add more definition to the foreground mountain and valley. Suggest the fir trees on the left and paint the dark area between the first two mountains. Finally, paint the dark hill on the bottom right.

Yellow Ochre + Hooker's Green Dark
+ Alizarin Crimson + French Ultramarine

Misty mountains

This is possibly one of the most common mountain images – behind mist and cloud. It has drama and atmosphere and is very exciting to paint. In this exercise, I used the lifting-out technique a great deal to help create the misty look.

❶ Draw the mountain outlines with your 2B pencil. Paint a wash from top to bottom, changing the colour as you work wet-on-wet.

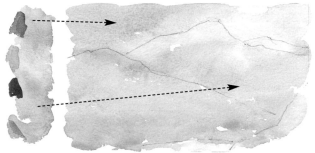

French Ultramarine
+ Yellow Ochre
+ Alizarin Crimson
+ Hooker's Green Dark

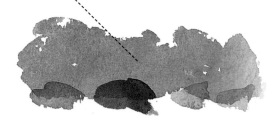

❷ Paint in the mountains and the valley. Create the mist and cloud effect by lifting out. I used diagonal brush strokes to give the impression of rain in the lower left of the painting.

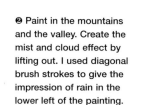

French Ultramarine + Alizarin Crimson
+ Yellow Ochre + Hooker's Green Dark

Snow-covered mountains

I painted the sky warm in this painting to suggest an afternoon in late winter. I have left white unpainted paper to show the majority of snow on the mountain. Always make sure that you leave plenty of paper to show snow; you can always paint over it later if you have left too much.

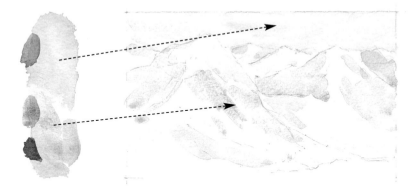

Yellow Ochre
+ Coeruleum
+ Alizarin Crimson

❶ Paint the sky up to and on to some mountains. When this is dry, paint in the snow shadows, making sure your brush strokes follow the slopes of the mountain downwards.

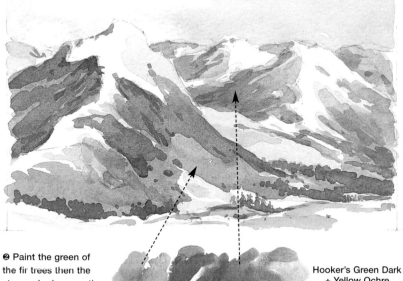

❷ Paint the green of the fir trees then the strong shadows on the mountains. When this is dry, use your small brush to paint in some darker modelling on the mountains and the fir trees in the valley.

Hooker's Green Dark
+ Yellow Ochre
+ Alizarin Crimson
+ Coeruleum

People in landscape

People add interest and can help to animate even the most ordinary landscape. This section is not about learning how to draw people as you would in a life class, but how to simplify them in order to bring your watercolour landscapes to life.

People talking

People usually communicate with each other, even if they are just passing the time of day. Therefore we must try to convey this in our paintings.

▶ Here are five bald heads. Below them I have added hair by painting just one brush stroke, making them look in definite directions. I have not added any features to the faces.

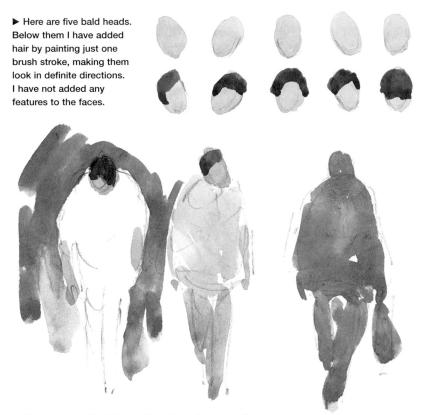

▲ The person on the left is looking down; the one in the centre is looking at the person in silhouette on the right. You will find you paint many silhouette figures in landscapes. Keep your figures simple; don't be tempted to overwork them.

Sketching figures

Painting people, like other subjects, requires practice. On these two pages are sketches that I have done from life and photographs. When you paint from life you will have to learn to work very fast as people move about. But remember that you are not looking for detail. When you work from a photograph, you must still keep the figures very simple. If you don't, they will be too carefully painted for you to add to your landscapes.

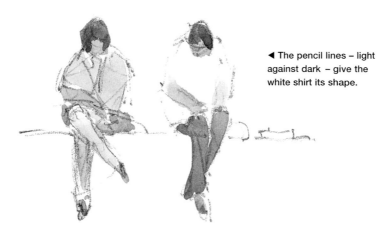

◀ The pencil lines – light against dark – give the white shirt its shape.

▼ This time the white shirt on the centre figure is helped by the orange figure.

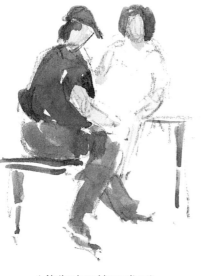

▲ Notice how I haven't put features onto the faces.

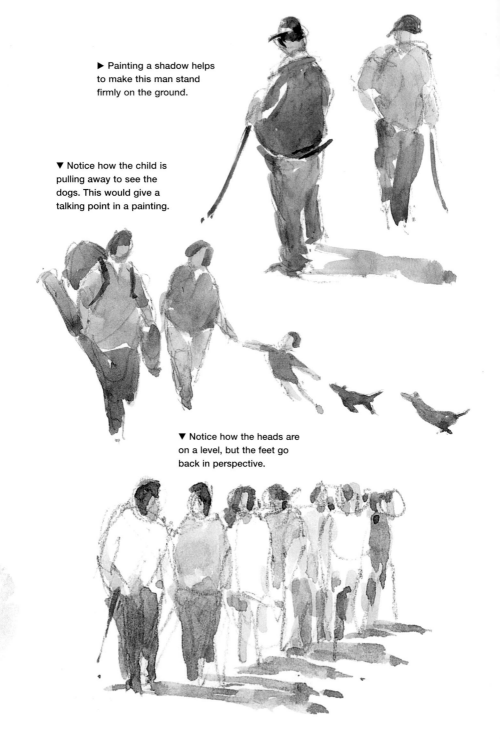

▶ Painting a shadow helps to make this man stand firmly on the ground.

▼ Notice how the child is pulling away to see the dogs. This would give a talking point in a painting.

▼ Notice how the heads are on a level, but the feet go back in perspective.

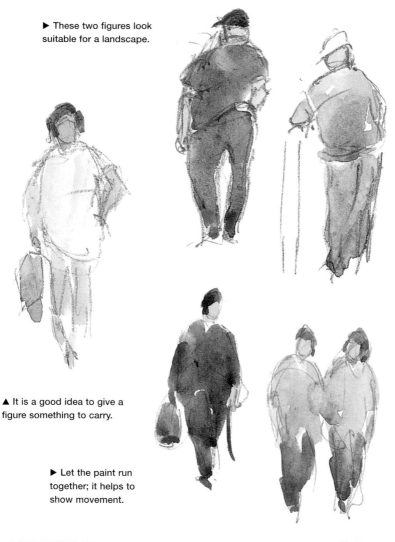

► These two figures look suitable for a landscape.

▲ It is a good idea to give a figure something to carry.

► Let the paint run together; it helps to show movement.

MUST KNOW

Copying photographs

A good way to start painting people is to copy photographs – they don't move! Make them very simple like your sketches. Give yourself a time limit; start by allowing yourself two minutes, then reduce it to one minute and, finally, just 30 seconds or less. You will be surprised at how fast you can sketch! Do not add detail and do not paint them any larger than the ones on these pages. When you are happy with the results, paint them from life but keep them simple.

Animals in landscape

Animals can add atmosphere to your landscapes. However, they will not pose for you to paint, so you must sketch as much as you can from life and take photographs to work from later. Be careful to keep an eye on their scale, especially when painting small animals, such as chickens or rabbits, as it is easy to paint them too large for the surrounding landscape.

Cows in a field

I drew these three cows from a group of ten that I had photographed, and put them in an imaginary landscape. Notice how the left cow stands out because its back is white against the dark trees. When cows are looking at you, you will see their typical expression of mournful curiosity!

▼ The background was painted first, then the dark trees and cows. The grass was added in two washes, using single brush strokes to represent its movement.

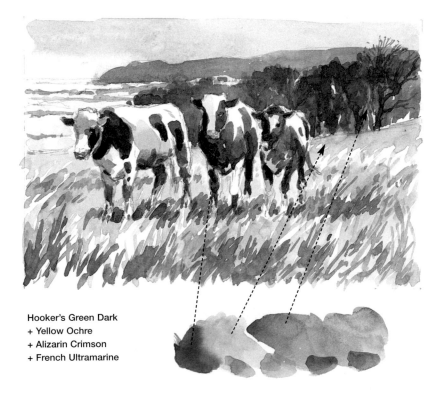

Hooker's Green Dark
+ Yellow Ochre
+ Alizarin Crimson
+ French Ultramarine

Sheep

Sheep are easy to draw and paint. In the distance, they can be suggested by small areas of unpainted paper. Close up, they may be simplified as an oblong box with four thin poles for legs and an oval-shaped head.

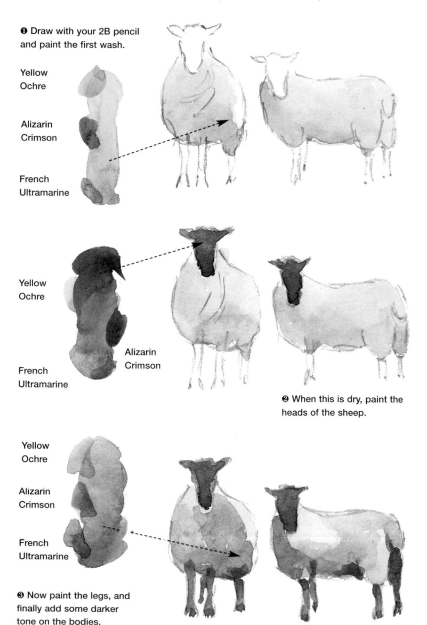

❶ Draw with your 2B pencil and paint the first wash.

Yellow Ochre

Alizarin Crimson

French Ultramarine

Yellow Ochre

French Ultramarine

Alizarin Crimson

❷ When this is dry, paint the heads of the sheep.

Yellow Ochre

Alizarin Crimson

French Ultramarine

❸ Now paint the legs, and finally add some darker tone on the bodies.

Cow

You may be lucky and find a cow that will stay in this position for three or four minutes, long enough for you to do a quick sketch. Do try sketching from life, as it will teach you a tremendous amount. Cows give a landscape painting a sense of serenity and well-being.

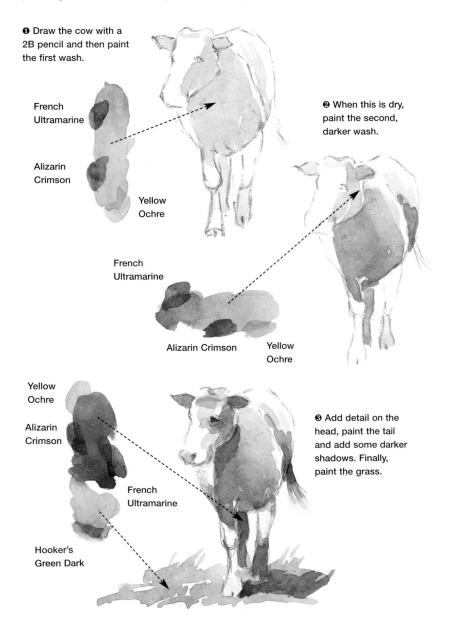

❶ Draw the cow with a 2B pencil and then paint the first wash.

French Ultramarine

Alizarin Crimson

Yellow Ochre

❷ When this is dry, paint the second, darker wash.

French Ultramarine

Alizarin Crimson

Yellow Ochre

Yellow Ochre

Alizarin Crimson

French Ultramarine

Hooker's Green Dark

❸ Add detail on the head, paint the tail and add some darker shadows. Finally, paint the grass.

Pony

I sketched this pony when it was tethered to a horsebox at a horse show. It looks as though it has been working hard and is now resting, or is thinking of the work it still has to do! Including horses in your landscapes will suggest work is being done on the land.

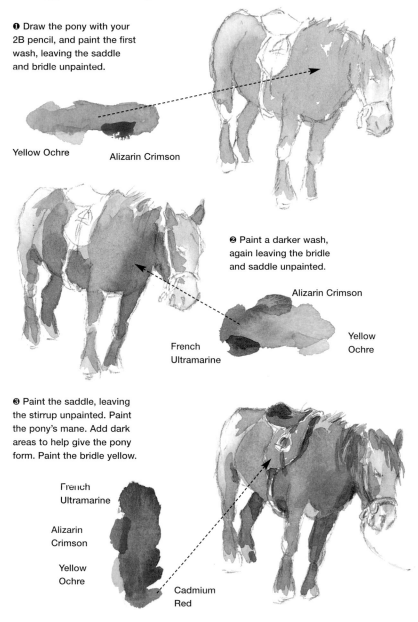

❶ Draw the pony with your 2B pencil, and paint the first wash, leaving the saddle and bridle unpainted.

Yellow Ochre   Alizarin Crimson

❷ Paint a darker wash, again leaving the bridle and saddle unpainted.

Alizarin Crimson

French Ultramarine

Yellow Ochre

❸ Paint the saddle, leaving the stirrup unpainted. Paint the pony's mane. Add dark areas to help give the pony form. Paint the bridle yellow.

French Ultramarine

Alizarin Crimson

Yellow Ochre

Cadmium Red

EXERCISE   ## Paint a rural landscape

In this exercise, the cows and the relaxed attitude of the man give the painting the feeling of a perfect summer's day. Remember that even small paintings like this one, which I painted the same size as it is reproduced here, can convey feelings to the onlooker.

The palette

| French Ultramarine | Cadmium Yellow Pale | Hooker's Green Dark | Alizarin Crimson |

PAINTING LANDSCAPES

① Draw the scene with your 2B pencil, and, using your small brush, paint the sky. Notice how one or two small areas are left unpainted, to show clouds.

French Ultramarine

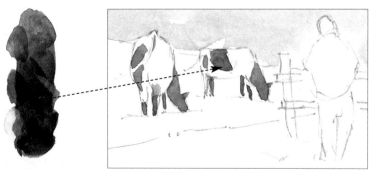

French Ultramarine
+ Alizarin Crimson
+ Cadmium Yellow Pale

② Using your small brush, paint the black markings on the cows, following the contours of the bodies.

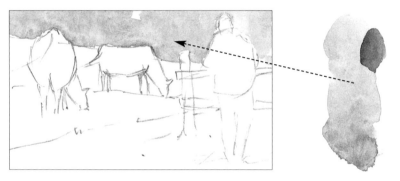

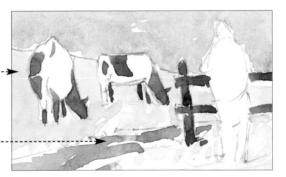

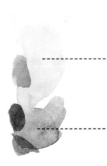

Cadmium Yellow Pale
+ Hooker's Green Dark
+ Alizarin Crimson
+ French Ultramarine

❸ Paint the grass and path. When this is dry, paint the fence, leaving the man as white paper.

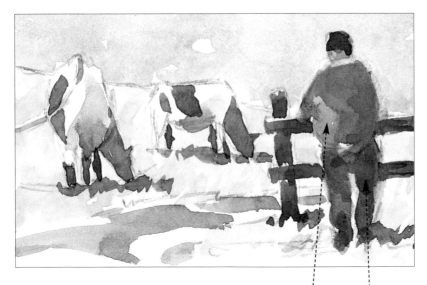

❹ Paint the man and then add some simple shadows on the cows and the cast shadows on the grass.

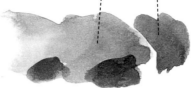

Cadmium Yellow Pale + Alizarin Crimson
+ French Ultramarine

Buildings

You can paint hundreds of perfect landscapes without putting in one building. But buildings, like animals and people, can add interest to a landscape. In their simplest form they are just like the box you practised painting on page 24. To simplify them to start with, try to imagine them as building blocks.

Farmhouse

This farmhouse in its simplest form is a box with a roof. The porch is also a box. The three-dimensional look came by adding shadows. The church is painted very simply; it is just a silhouette with no detail. This is another way to make buildings simple to draw and paint.

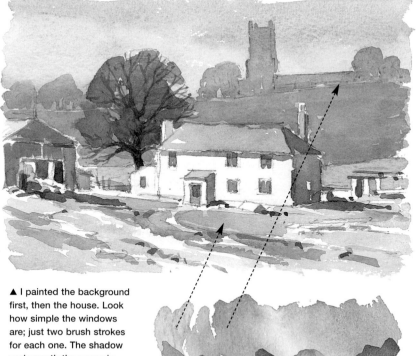

▲ I painted the background first, then the house. Look how simple the windows are; just two brush strokes for each one. The shadow underneath the eaves is important as it makes the roof stand out from the wall. Remember that shadows create form and show shape.

Hooker's Green Dark + Cadmium Red + Alizarin Crimson + Yellow Ochre + French Ultramarine

Simplified buildings

If you are working from a photograph, middle-distance buildings will usually look smaller than in real life. This is natural when you use a camera. Your eyes see the buildings larger as they unconsciously close in on them.

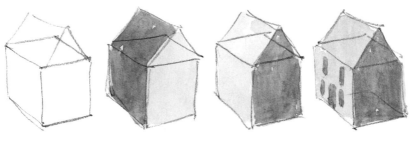

▲ Here you can see how light against dark defines the shape of the building.

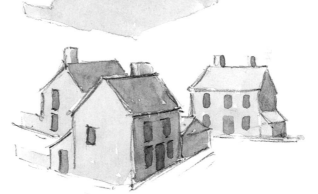

▶ The yellow painted area is a meaningless shape. However, if you add some shadows it becomes a group of houses.

▼ Painting buildings in silhouette makes them easier to portray. The only detail in this sketch is the three windows.

Mediterranean farmhouse

This is a very easy farmhouse to draw. It is made up of just four boxes. The cypress trees behind help to define the outline shape, light against dark. Notice how the windows on this building are simple dark brush strokes.

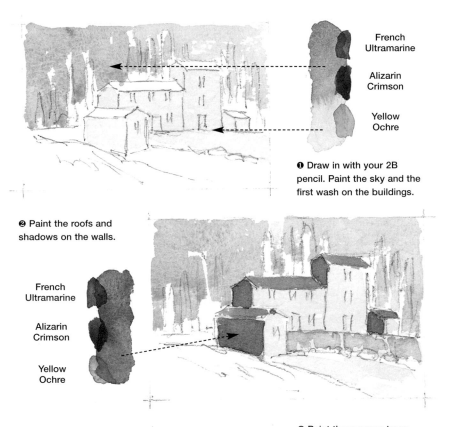

French
Ultramarine

Alizarin
Crimson

Yellow
Ochre

❶ Draw in with your 2B pencil. Paint the sky and the first wash on the buildings.

❷ Paint the roofs and shadows on the walls.

French
Ultramarine

Alizarin
Crimson

Yellow
Ochre

❸ Paint the cypress trees, darken the wall and put in the windows. Finally, add some foreground.

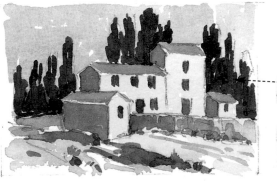

French
Ultramarine

Alizarin
Crimson

Hooker's
Green Dark

Row of houses

This group of houses is more complicated to paint than the last exercise. But study the painting carefully and you can see how it is still made up of light and dark areas. If you practise I am sure you will be able to paint this well.

❶ Draw in with your 2B pencil. Paint in the sky and the first wash on the buildings. When the sky is dry, paint the tree.

❷ Paint the shadows and windows. Paint the ground wet-on-wet, and paint up onto the main house wall to give it character. Add grass detail. Paint in the telegraph pole and smaller tree.

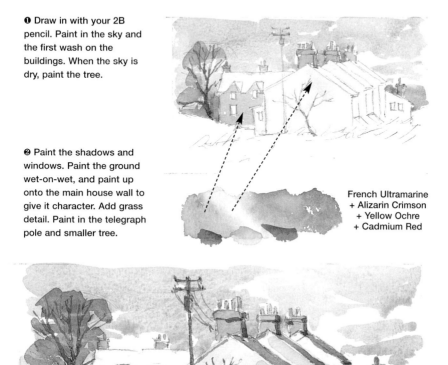

French Ultramarine
+ Alizarin Crimson
+ Yellow Ochre
+ Cadmium Red

Yellow Ochre
+ Alizarin Crimson
+ Hooker's Green Dark
+ French Ultramarine

Sketching buildings and other features

Always carry a sketchbook with you to record objects you see outdoors.
You can sketch a full scene or a small detail such as a leaf, a branch or a
gate. If you have a camera with you, take a photo of the objects you
sketch. This will teach you a great deal about working from photographs,
especially about how the camera sees things and how you see them and
sketch them. Photographs are a great source of information and
inspiration when you are working indoors.

▶ The first two sketches
are painted very simply to
show the situation of the
buildings. They could be
used as a focal point in
a larger painting.

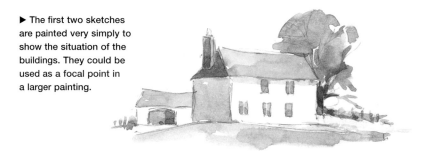

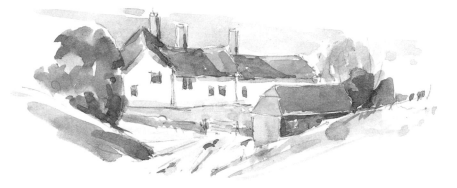

▼ This painting is a little more
complicated. The water is very
simple yet effective.

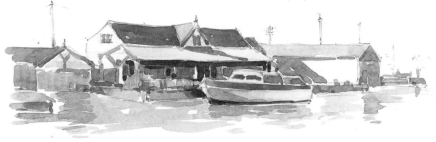

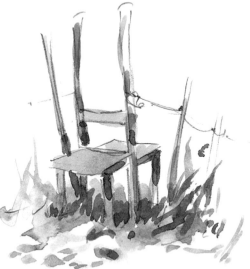

▼ This sketch of a stile is useful to practise.

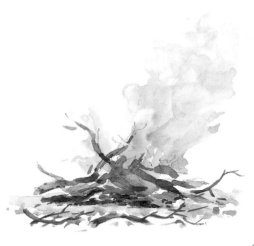

▲ The smoke and flames from this fire were painted wet-on-wet after the branches were painted.

▲ Seagulls on a ploughed field are a common sight in a landscape. My sketch looks complicated but most of it is suggested, leaving white areas for the distant seagulls and only adding details in the foreground.

want to know more?

Take it to the next level...

Go to...

▶ **Seas** – page 94
▶ **People on the beach** – page 116
▶ **Composition** – page 156

Other sources

▶ **Sketchbooks**
   essential for improving observational skills
▶ **Society for All Artists (SAA)**
   membership benefits and newsletter
▶ **Local art club or society**
   you may need to be a member
▶ **Museums and art galleries**
   good sources of inspiration
▶ **Publications**
   visit www.collins.co.uk for Collins art books

painting the

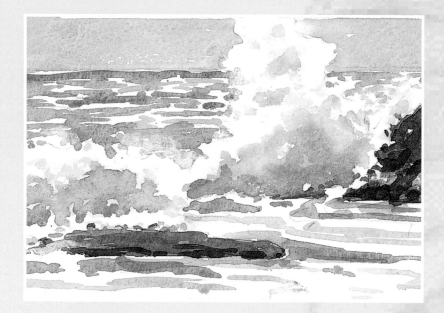

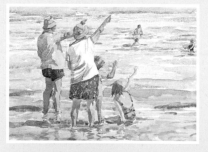

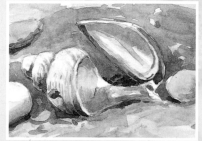

seashore

The seashore is a wonderful place to paint. It can be exciting in the summer when the beaches are crowded with holidaymakers, or in winter when the sea is rough and the sky is changing constantly. In any season, it is relaxing to pick up shells or look for a place to paint. Your paintings can be memorable keepsakes, and your sketches good reference.

Techniques

Here are some exciting techniques that will help you become a fully fledged seashore artist. You will get to know your brushes and paints and the effects you can achieve with them.

Dry brush

How can you paint with a dry brush? Well, it isn't actually dry, just dryer than normal, so if you drag the brush along the paper the paint hits and misses as it goes along, leaving some white paper showing. This gives a lovely sparkly effect which is very good for painting water or pebbles on the beach. This technique is more effective on rough-surfaced paper.

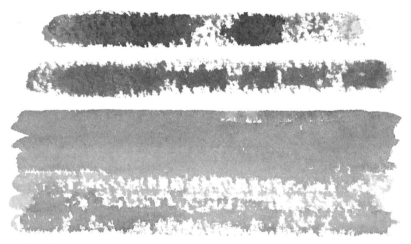

▲ Here, the dry-brush technique is used to show sunlight sparkling on the sea.

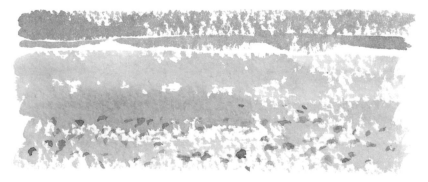

▲ A few darker marks over dry-brush 'sand' give the impression of pebbles on a beach.

Using a rigger brush

The hairs on a rigger brush are long and thin and all the same length. This enables a brush full of wet paint to continue producing the same thickness of line for a long time. The less pressure you use, the thinner the line will be. A rigger is mainly used for painting the rigging on boats, but it is useful wherever you need to paint fine lines.

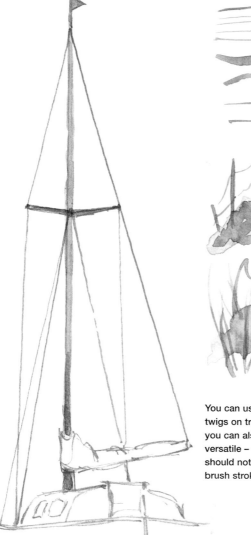

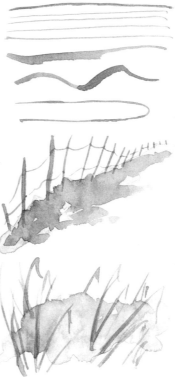

You can use a rigger for fences, grasses, twigs on trees, the rigging on boats, and you can also draw with it. It is extremely versatile – a fabulous brush – and you should not be without one. Practise these brush strokes and experiment for yourself.

Blotting out with a tissue

Blotting out is another technique used to remove paint from your picture, but unlike lifting out, where the original paint has to be dry, when you use the blotting-out technique the paint must be wet. A rolled-up tissue is used to remove areas of wet paint. Blotting out is more spontaneous than lifting out, which makes it a more suitable technique for soft subjects with irregular outlines such as the clouds and waves shown below.

▶ Paint in the blue sky, leaving some paper white. Screw up a tissue and, while the sky is still wet, blot out some cloud shapes. When dry, paint in the cloud shadows.

▲ Add a little green to blue and paint in the sea, leaving some white unpainted paper. While this is still wet, blot out the spray on the waves with a tissue, then paint in the sand.

PAINTING THE SEASHORE

Shadows

Shadows are important in a painting, as they add sunshine and life. To paint them successfully, all you have to know is how to mix the shadow colour and where the light is coming from. Shadows vary in length at different times of day, and are darker or lighter depending on the strength of the light. They also help to make objects look three dimensional.

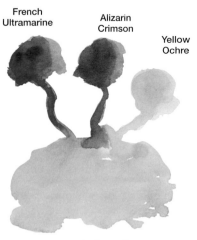

French
Ultramarine

Alizarin
Crimson

Yellow
Ochre

= shadow colour

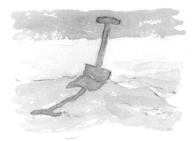

▲ Here the sun is coming from behind the spade stuck into the sand.

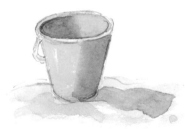

▲ The sun is shining from the left of this bucket in the sand.

▲ Because watercolour is transparent, when you paint the shadow colour the underneath colour will show through, but darker, giving the illusion of a shadow.

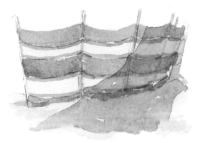

▲ This picture shows a shadow cast by another object, falling on a windbreak.

▶ # Shells and pebbles

You can find an amazing selection of shells and pebbles on the beach. They have interesting shapes and wonderful colours. You can paint or draw them where you find them, or take them home to work from. Either way, this is a simple but rewarding subject to practise with your watercolours.

Broken shells

This painting has been included to give you inspiration, and to show how just a few varied pebbles and shells can make an interesting painting. Next time you are on the beach, look out for these 'ready-made' subjects.

▲ The pale yellow sand was painted wet-on-wet around the pebbles and shells. These were painted next, leaving unpainted paper for highlights. When the background was dry, the dark sand colour was painted to help define the shapes of the shells and pebbles. Finally, the shadows were added to them and their cast shadows on the sand.

French Ultramarine + Alizarin Crimson +Yellow Ochre + Cadmium Yellow Pale

Pebbles

When someone says 'paint a pebble' it sounds very uninspiring. But take a closer look at pebbles and you will find beautiful colours and patterns on them. I am always delighted with the pebbles I find on the beach. They are an easy subject for a beginner, because they are such simple shapes.

❶ These two pebbles have elegant shapes. Draw them with your 2B pencil. Using your small brush, paint the large one soft grey, the other pale yellow with a little grey, wet-on-wet.

❷ Paint the rings on the large pebble and let it dry. Then paint the shadows on both pebbles.

❸ Paint the cast shadows on the ground, leaving a thin white highlight underneath both of the pebbles.

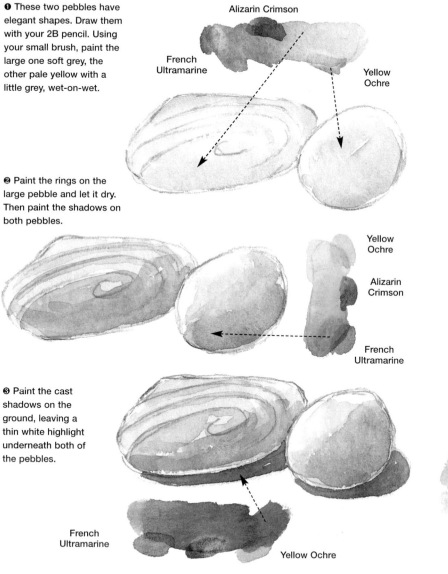

Alizarin Crimson

French Ultramarine

Yellow Ochre

Yellow Ochre

Alizarin Crimson

French Ultramarine

French Ultramarine

Yellow Ochre

Alizarin Crimson

Scallop shell

This shell is shaped like a fan. Don't worry if yours is a little different to the one shown below; concentrate on the ridges and the dark pink lines around the shell as they are important, helping to give it its familiar form.

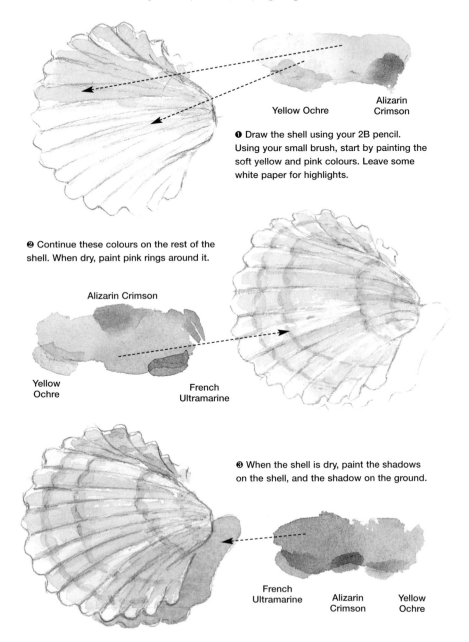

Yellow Ochre

Alizarin Crimson

❶ Draw the shell using your 2B pencil. Using your small brush, start by painting the soft yellow and pink colours. Leave some white paper for highlights.

❷ Continue these colours on the rest of the shell. When dry, paint pink rings around it.

Alizarin Crimson

Yellow Ochre

French Ultramarine

❸ When the shell is dry, paint the shadows on the shell, and the shadow on the ground.

French Ultramarine

Alizarin Crimson

Yellow Ochre

PAINTING THE SEASHORE

Sketching shells

Sketching shells on the beach is almost as easy as painting indoors. The shells don't move, and if you are lucky with the weather you have plenty of time to sketch them. Try copying these sketches. Note how the darks and lights give the shells form and help them to look three dimensional.

▼ This is an easily recognizable shell shape.

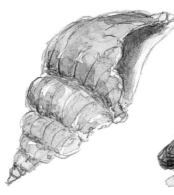

▶ The shadow helps to sit this shell on the ground.

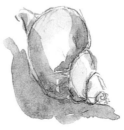

◀ This mussel was painted wet-on-wet. The darks and lights give it its oval shape.

▼ Here is another good subject for a painting which can be found 'ready-made' on the beach.

MUST KNOW

Making individual shells important

Paint them dark against a light-coloured background or paint them light against a dark-coloured background. Make some of the background shells less distinct and the nearest shells and foreground stronger. This will make them appear nearer and more important. Adding shadows will help to make shells appear three-dimensional.

EXERCISE **Paint shells and pebbles**

By making sure the shells and pebbles are not too crowded together, you can see their distinct shapes, making them easier to paint. Background pebbles are kept less distinct to create the impression of distance.

The palette

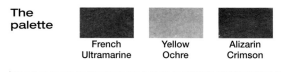

French Ultramarine | Yellow Ochre | Alizarin Crimson

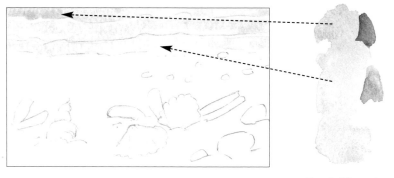

❶ Draw the scene with your 2B pencil, then paint in the sea using your large brush, wet-on-wet.

French Ultramarine + Yellow Ochre

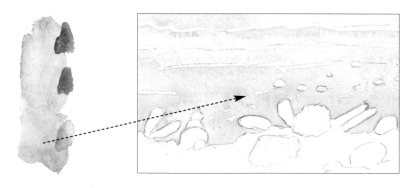

French Ultramarine + Alizarin Crimson + Yellow Ochre

❷ Carry on painting the sea wet-on-wet and continue into the sand around the pebbles and shells.

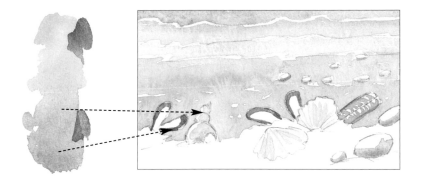

Alizarin Crimson
+ French Ultramarine

❸ When dry, start painting the pebbles and shells with your small brush, leaving some unpainted paper for highlights.

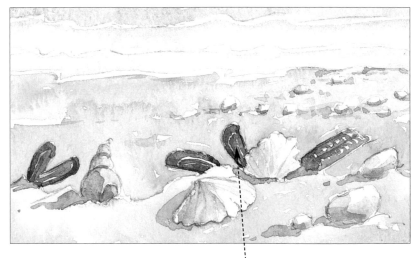

❹ Paint the foreground sand around the shells and pebbles. Add more colour to these, let them dry, then add shadows.

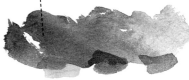

Yellow Ochre + Alizarin Crimson
+ French Ultramarine

▶ Marine life

Many living creatures are found at the seaside. This section illustrates a few of the fascinating crustaceans, seaweeds and fish you may see. After practising painting these, you will be able to paint many others of your own choice. You can also practise painting different types from photographs.

Crabs

Crabs are some of the most commonly seen creatures on the seashore. You will find them in all sorts of environments: in tiny rock pools, under pebbles and in the open sea. They vary greatly in shape, size and colour. Their subtle colouring makes them fascinating for an artist to paint.

▲ First, the sand around the crabs was painted wet-on-wet. When this was dry, the crabs themselves were painted, varying the colours. Once dry, the shadows on the shells and stones were added. Finally, the cast shadows were painted on the sand.

Yellow Ochre + Alizarin Crimson + French Ultramarine

Prawn

We are used to seeing pink prawns, but they are this colour only after they have been cooked. The prawns that we see in rock pools are generally similar in colour to the one painted here. You will find that your rigger brush comes in useful for painting the prawn's long feelers.

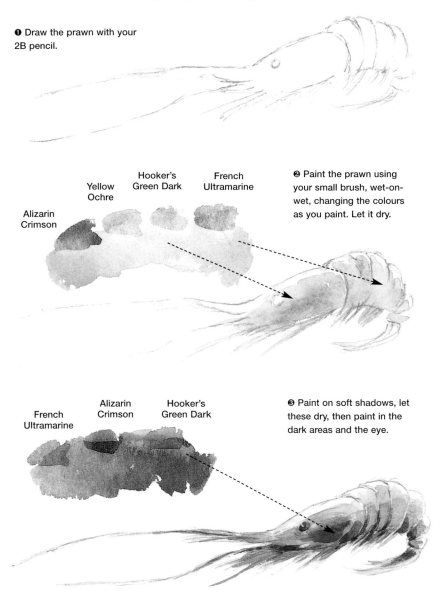

❶ Draw the prawn with your 2B pencil.

Alizarin Crimson

Yellow Ochre

Hooker's Green Dark

French Ultramarine

❷ Paint the prawn using your small brush, wet-on-wet, changing the colours as you paint. Let it dry.

French Ultramarine

Alizarin Crimson

Hooker's Green Dark

❸ Paint on soft shadows, let these dry, then paint in the dark areas and the eye.

Starfish

Walking on your local beach, you may be amazed at how many starfish there are. Photograph one in its natural setting and then use this to paint from at home. The shape and the colours will make an interesting painting.

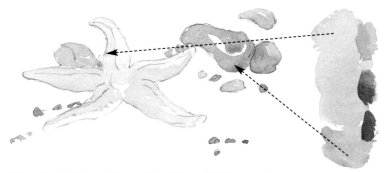

❶ Draw the starfish and stones with a 2B pencil. With a small brush, paint the starfish with a pale wash, leaving some white unpainted paper. Paint the grey stones, leaving highlights on the large one. Paint the orange stones and leave to dry.

Yellow Ochre
+ Alizarin Crimson
+ French Ultramarine

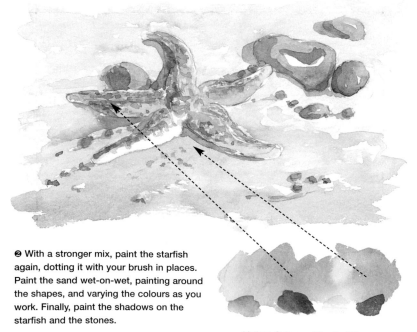

❷ With a stronger mix, paint the starfish again, dotting it with your brush in places. Paint the sand wet-on-wet, painting around the shapes, and varying the colours as you work. Finally, paint the shadows on the starfish and the stones.

Yellow Ochre + Alizarin Crimson
+ Cadmium Yellow Pale + French Ultramarine

Seaweed

This is just one of the many varieties of seaweed found on the seashore. Seaweeds are many colours; browns, yellows, reds and greens. They are usually very different colours when wet and when dry. Sketch different seaweeds next time you are on the beach, or take them home to sketch.

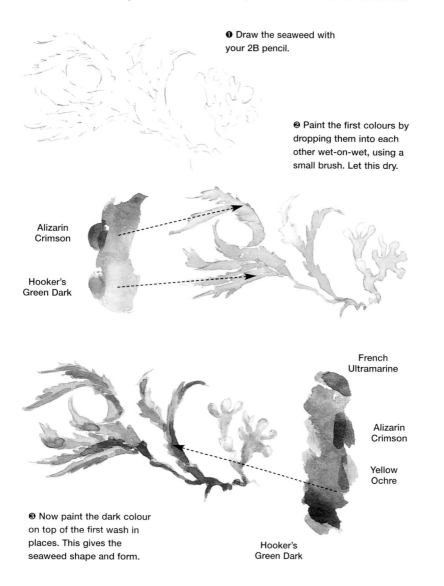

❶ Draw the seaweed with your 2B pencil.

❷ Paint the first colours by dropping them into each other wet-on-wet, using a small brush. Let this dry.

Alizarin Crimson

Hooker's Green Dark

French Ultramarine

Alizarin Crimson

Yellow Ochre

❸ Now paint the dark colour on top of the first wash in places. This gives the seaweed shape and form.

Hooker's Green Dark

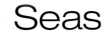

Seas

Water is wonderful to paint, especially the sea. Its moods and colours change constantly. From a large seascape to a close-up of a wave, it is an inspiring and challenging subject. Enjoy copying these exercises; they will give you a glimpse of the many opportunities the sea has to offer an artist.

Swelling sea

The painting below shows the many colours and patterns that you can find in the sea. The colours will change with the reflections on the sea when the sunlight is shining through it. They will also vary depending on what is hidden underneath the surface.

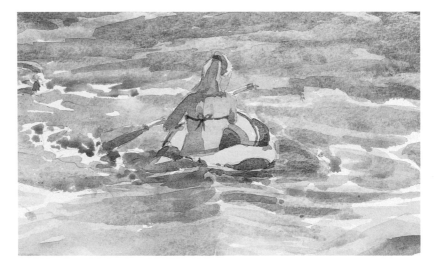

▲ Paint the sea first, leaving the girl, the boat and the movement lines in the water as unpainted paper. When dry, paint the girl and the boat and then the reflections on the water. When this is dry, paint in all the shadows. Notice the simplicity of the shadow on the girl and of the water itself; don't be tempted to overwork it.

MUST KNOW

Painting waves
Leave the foam of the waves as white paper, and make the shadows under the waves dark. You can always 'lift out' the paint (see page 19) if these areas are too dark.

Waves breaking on a beach

Waves can change colour and shape according to the weather, the type of sea bed lying underneath and when they are crashing onto rocks. Always leave plenty of white paper for the foam, you can paint over it if you have left too much. In this painting, the waves are breaking onto a beach.

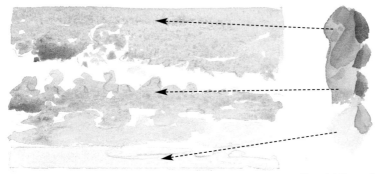

❶ Draw in the basic shapes with a 2B pencil. Then, using your large brush, paint the sea as a graded wash, leaving some white paper for the foam.

French Ultramarine
+ Alizarin Crimson
+ Hooker's Green Dark
+ Yellow Ochre

❷ When dry, mix a shadow colour. Paint behind the wave, leaving some underpainting showing. Continue painting shadows on the wave. Finally, soften some areas by lifting out.

Yellow Ochre + Hooker's Green Dark
+ Alizarin Crimson + French Ultramarine

Calm sea

In the painting below, this is a totally different sea to the one depicted on the previous page. It is more the colour found around a tropical island, and the overall atmosphere is extremely tranquil. This is a perfect example of water painted very simply, without overworking.

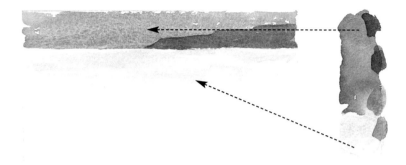

❶ Paint the sky using your large brush. When it is dry, paint the headland with your small brush. Let that dry and then start painting a wash for the sea.

French Ultramarine
+ Alizarin Crimson
+ Coeruleum
+ Yellow Ochre

❷ Continue painting the sea, leaving white paper for the waves. Paint the sand, leaving some unpainted lines leading to the sea. When dry, paint in the horizontal shadows under the waves and the dark lines on the beach.

Alizarin Crimson
+ Yellow Ochre + Coeruleum

Waves crashing on rocks

This is a lively scene with waves crashing onto rocks, throwing up lots of spray. The colour of the sea, the sparkling white of the waves and the dark rocks make the painting vibrant, and the contrast of the very dark areas with the white paper adds dimension and drama.

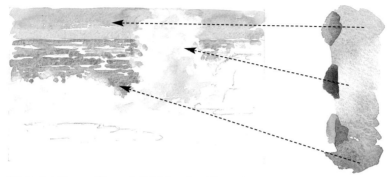

❶ Draw in with your 2B pencil. Paint the sky with your large brush, leaving the wave unpainted. Then paint the sea, leaving small white horizontal areas for the background waves. Add soft shadows to the spray.

French Ultramarine
+ Alizarin Crimson
+ Hooker's Green Dark

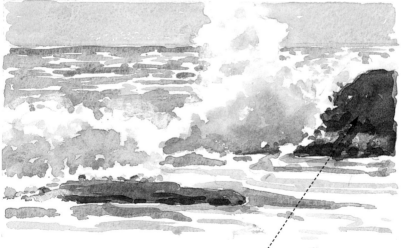

❷ Paint the dark rocks, leaving little specks of white paper to suggest spray. Paint darker areas on the spray, wet-on-wet. Then paint the sea around the rocks with horizontal brush strokes.

Hooker's Green Dark
+ Alizarin Crimson + French Ultramarine

EXERCISE ## Paint a seascape

When you paint this scene, the first two stages are painted while the paint is still wet, so don't stop in the middle, just keep going. Your colours may vary from mine, because they will merge differently when they are wet.

The palette

Coeruleum   French Ultramarine   Alizarin Crimson   Yellow Ochre

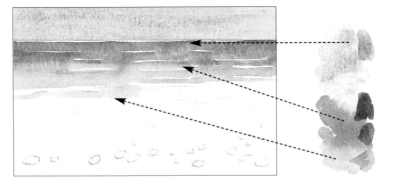

❶ Using your large brush, paint the sky and sea, leaving a thin unpainted line on the horizon. This prevents the sea merging into the sky.

Coeruleum
+ Alizarin Crimson
+ French Ultramarine
+ Yellow Ochre

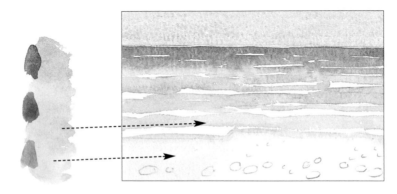

French Ultramarine
+ Alizarin Crimson
+ Yellow Ochre

❷ Paint the sea and the sand, using the graded wash technique. Leave horizontal white paper lines for the waves.

❸ Finish painting the sand. When it is dry, paint the shadows under the waves. Leave to dry.

French Ultramarine
+ Alizarin Crimson
+ Yellow Ochre

❹ Use your small brush to paint in the darker sand, leaving the stones pale yellow. When dry, paint in the shadows on the stones.

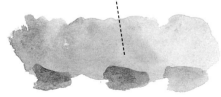

French Ultramarine + Alizarin Crimson
+ Yellow Ochre

Cliffs and rocks

Cliffs and rocks play an important role when you are painting the seashore. They give scale and stability to a seascape painting. They can also help you to paint a recognizable place, especially if they have very distinctive shapes. Cliffs also vary in colour depending on the underlying rock.

Cliffs in silhouette

This is one of many ways of painting cliffs, looking towards the sun. The cliffs become silhouettes and the sea is so bright, it is almost white. You can hardly see the green of the trees and fields on the cliff, and the cliff itself is too dark in shadow to see its colours.

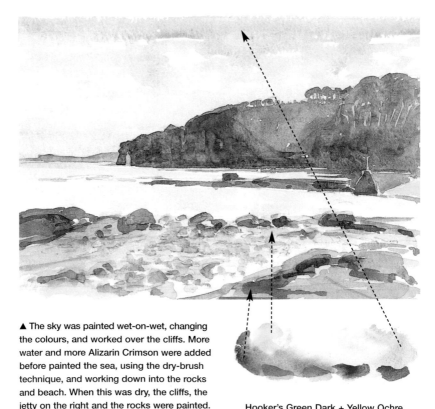

▲ The sky was painted wet-on-wet, changing the colours, and worked over the cliffs. More water and more Alizarin Crimson were added before painted the sea, using the dry-brush technique, and working down into the rocks and beach. When this was dry, the cliffs, the jetty on the right and the rocks were painted. When this was dry, shadows were added.

Hooker's Green Dark + Yellow Ochre + Alizarin Crimson + French Ultramarine

Distant cliffs

Look carefully at the shapes and colours of cliffs before you start to draw
and paint them. Just a few minutes spent looking and observing all the
details will help your painting to be believable and give you confidence.

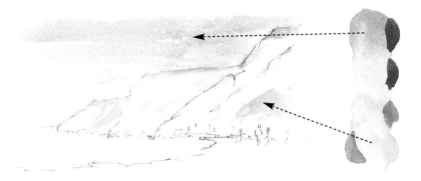

❶ Draw the scene with your 2B pencil. Paint the sky with
your large brush, going over the far cliff and the sea using
the dry-brush technique. Paint the greens on the cliffs,
using warmer colours on the nearest cliff.

French Ultramarine
+ Alizarin Crimson
+ Hooker's Green Dark
+ Yellow Ochre

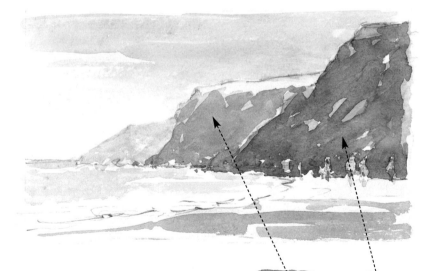

❷ When dry, use your small brush to paint
soft, warm shadows on the far cliff, bluer on
the middle cliff and add more red and green
paint on the nearest cliff, leaving white
shapes for the figures. Add more colour to
the sea and sand. Finally, paint the figures.

French Ultramarine + Alizarin Crimson
+ Yellow Ochre + Hooker's Green Dark

Rocks

Rocks are in some ways just small versions of cliffs, or big versions of stones. The rocks in this painting are quite brightly coloured. In some places you will find they are grey, black or even green where seaweed has stuck to them.

❶ Draw the scene with your 2B pencil, and then paint the rocks using your small brush, leaving a thin unpainted line between them, so that the colours won't run from one rock into another.

Yellow Ochre

Alizarin Crimson

French Ultramarine

❷ When dry, paint in the sea, and then the sand.

French Ultramarine

Hooker's Green Dark

❸ Paint in the last rocks, let them dry, and paint the strong shadows and the rock formation lines.

Alizarin Crimson

Yellow Ochre

French Ultramarine

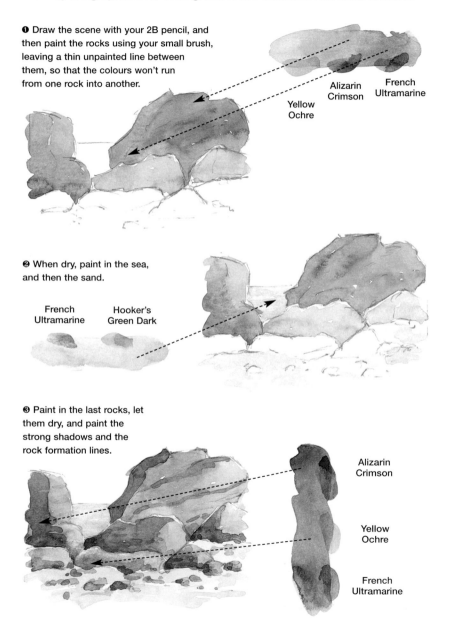

Rock pool

Rock pools are magical, miniature water worlds full of life, and children and adults alike love them. They can be large or very small. The colours vary according to the type of pool, what is in it, and the reflections on it.

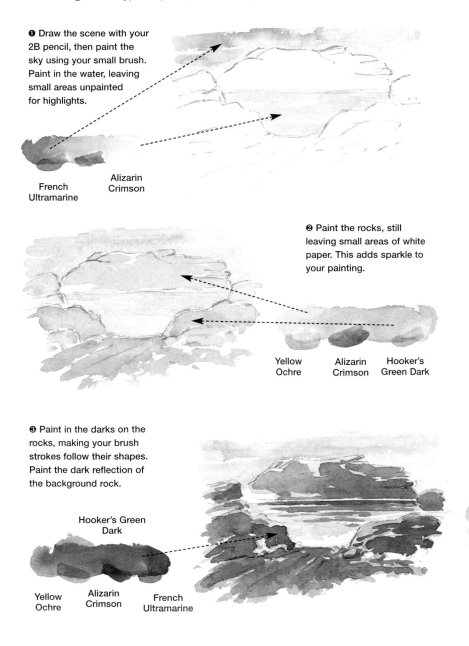

❶ Draw the scene with your 2B pencil, then paint the sky using your small brush. Paint in the water, leaving small areas unpainted for highlights.

French Ultramarine

Alizarin Crimson

❷ Paint the rocks, still leaving small areas of white paper. This adds sparkle to your painting.

Yellow Ochre

Alizarin Crimson

Hooker's Green Dark

❸ Paint in the darks on the rocks, making your brush strokes follow their shapes. Paint the dark reflection of the background rock.

Hooker's Green Dark

Yellow Ochre

Alizarin Crimson

French Ultramarine

Sea birds

The most easily recognized sea birds are the gulls. There are many different types and you will often see flocks of them soaring in the sky or groups scavenging on the beach. They will give life and movement to your seascapes.

Flying gulls

The painting below is very typical of a flock of seagulls 'playing' over the sea. A dark sky has been painted to emphasize the white shapes of the gulls. Don't attempt to add details to them because your eye will be drawn to individual birds rather than seeing the flight of the whole flock.

▲ The gulls were drawn with a 2B pencil. Then the sky was painted around them wet-on-wet. Specks of unpainted paper were left to give the impression of distant gulls. The gulls were painted with soft shadows. When this was dry, their legs and the tips of their wings were painted.

Yellow Ochre + Alizarin Crimson + French Ultramarine

Black-headed gull

When they are flying, birds are usually very graceful. Sometimes, however, especially if they are walking, they can look extremely comical, like the one painted here. It has a rather quizzical expression, as if it is asking for food.

Alizarin Crimson

Yellow Ochre

French Ultramarine

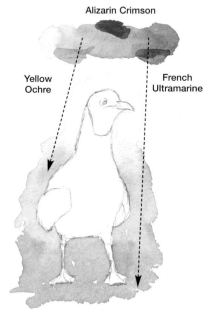

❶ Draw the gull carefully with a 2B pencil to get the shape right. Then paint around it with your small brush, wet-on-wet. Let this dry.

French Ultramarine

Alizarin Crimson

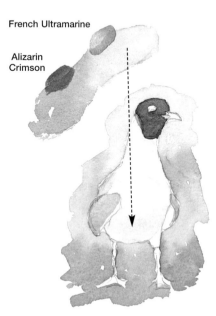

❷ Next paint the head, leaving the eye white. Paint the wings, and then paint in the soft shadow down the front of the bird.

French Ultramarine

Alizarin Crimson

Yellow Ochre

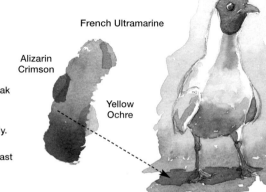

❸ When dry, paint the beak and legs, then stronger shadow under the chin, neck and front lower body. Paint the rest of the shadows, including the cast shadow on the ground. Finally, paint in the eye.

Curlew

Curlews are very distinctive with their long curved beaks and slender legs. This is a lovely shape to draw with long, flowing lines from the beak down under the chest and over the top of the beak to the tail.

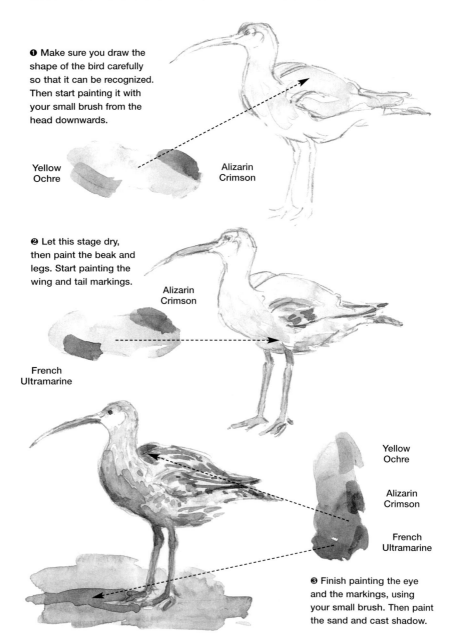

❶ Make sure you draw the shape of the bird carefully so that it can be recognized. Then start painting it with your small brush from the head downwards.

Yellow Ochre

Alizarin Crimson

❷ Let this stage dry, then paint the beak and legs. Start painting the wing and tail markings.

Alizarin Crimson

French Ultramarine

Yellow Ochre

Alizarin Crimson

French Ultramarine

❸ Finish painting the eye and the markings, using your small brush. Then paint the sand and cast shadow.

PAINTING THE SEASHORE

106

Sketching sea birds

Sketching birds out of doors is very difficult. They are constantly on the move and do not pose for long. But it is good practice and fun to have a go at sketching them. Don't worry if you only get parts of them, and don't forget that you can also take photographs and paint from these.

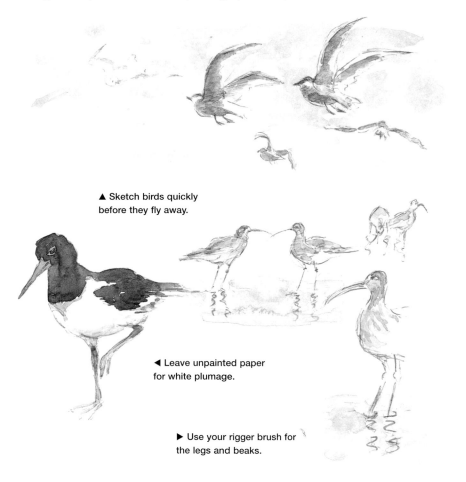

▲ Sketch birds quickly
before they fly away.

◀ Leave unpainted paper
for white plumage.

▶ Use your rigger brush for
the legs and beaks.

MUST KNOW

Sketching birds

If you are sketching a bird and it flies away, start another one – don't worry, it happens to all of us! Birds flying in the distance need only be simple shapes. When sketching a group, you need have only two or three carefully drawn birds in front; illusion will do the rest. Keep reflections very simple.

On the beach

In the summer the beach is full of exciting subjects to paint, from a simple windbreak, to a more complex donkey. Take each new subject as a challenge and enjoy having a go at painting many different things when you visit the seaside.

Sand dunes

This is part of a larger painting and shows some high sand dunes, which are topped with coarse grasses, and long stretches of sandy beach. In the summer, many families come to the dunes to picnic and holiday.

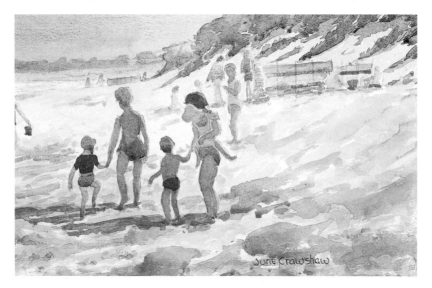

▲ The distant land and people were painted very soft and bluish to keep them in the background. The windbreaks and middle figures were painted in stronger colours, and the foreground people the strongest, giving depth and distance to the painting. Finally, some strong shadows were added to the foreground people and the beach to give the impression of sunlight.

MUST KNOW

Creating distance

Distant people are small but get larger as they get closer. Distant hills and cliffs are bluer or paler, getting stronger and brighter nearer the foreground. Shadows are stronger in bright sunlight.

Pebbly beach

Most beaches have some pebbles. Look carefully at the scene below, and see how simply they are painted. Most of them are merely suggested, with the use of magical shadows to make them appear three dimensional.

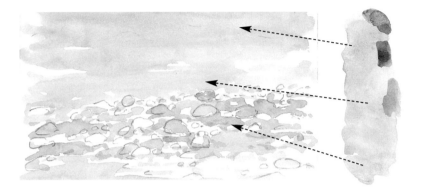

❶ Draw in a few pebbles with your 2B pencil, then paint the sand using your large brush and leave most of the pebble area as unpainted paper. When this is dry, paint in the grey and pink areas of the pebbles.

French Ultramarine
+ Alizarin Crimson
+ Yellow Ochre

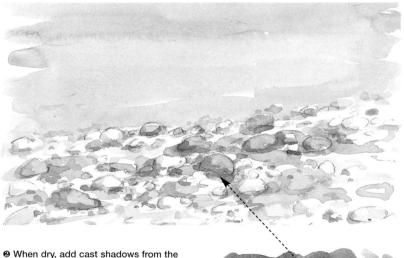

❷ When dry, add cast shadows from the pebbles, and paint a few darker pebbles in places. Don't copy my painting exactly; if you are happy with your results, that's fine.

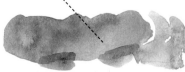

French Ultramarine
+ Alizarin Crimson + Yellow Ochre

Breakwater

Breakwaters can make interesting little paintings close up, like the one below, or they can be used as important elements in a larger seascape. They can look very new or may be worn away by the sea to almost nothing. They add interest and scale to a beach painting.

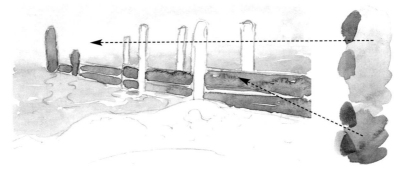

❶ Using your 2B pencil, draw in the scene. Then use your large brush to paint a blue-grey wash for the sky and the sea. Start painting in the breakwater.

French Ultramarine
+ Hooker's Green Dark
+ Alizarin Crimson
+ Yellow Ochre

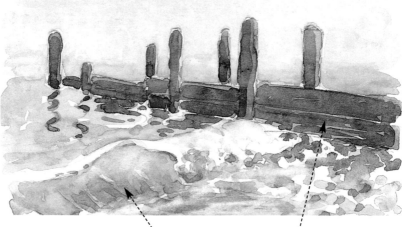

❷ Continue painting the breakwater. Paint the yellowish wave, leaving white paper for the spray, and continue up the beach. Paint the reflections in the water. Add darks where they are needed.

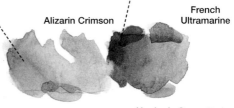

Alizarin Crimson

French Ultramarine

Yellow Ochre

Hooker's Green Dark

Beach huts

Beach huts are like brightly coloured little houses, and they add colour and life to a beach scene. Sometimes they are bleached by the sun and the sea, and look wonderfully weathered. This exercise, of a row of three beach huts, shows you how simply they can be painted.

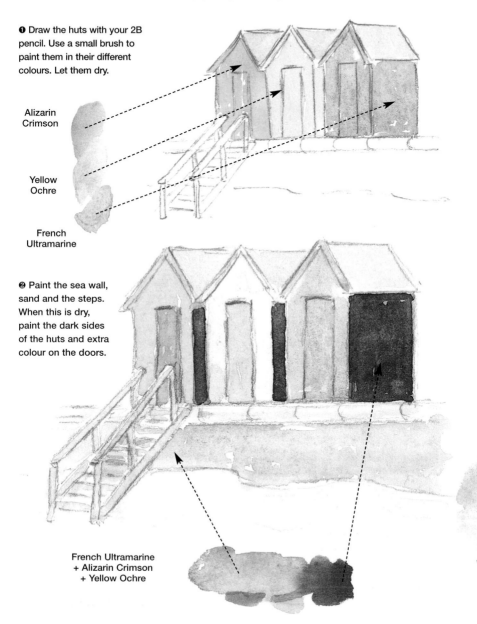

❶ Draw the huts with your 2B pencil. Use a small brush to paint them in their different colours. Let them dry.

Alizarin Crimson

Yellow Ochre

French Ultramarine

❷ Paint the sea wall, sand and the steps. When this is dry, paint the dark sides of the huts and extra colour on the doors.

French Ultramarine
+ Alizarin Crimson
+ Yellow Ochre

Sketching at the beach

Don't forget to take your sketchbook when you go to the beach. There is
always something for you to sketch. Practise by copying these pictures.
Notice how the beach huts below and the breakwater opposite are painted
more freely than those on the previous pages. This is because the sketches
are painted as part of a scene and not as objects in their own right.

▶ The shadows cast by
these beach huts show that
it is a sunny day.

◀ Note how the shadow of
the person is visible through
the deck chair.

▶ Windbreaks are simple to
sketch and very effective.

▼ These sand castles look
three dimensional because
of their shadows.

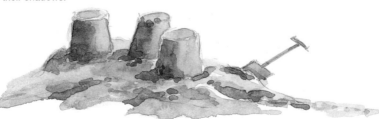

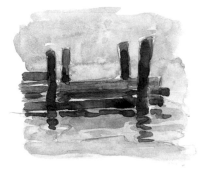

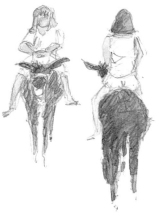

▲ Just one of the many
ways to paint a breakwater.

▲ Drawn and shaded with a
2B pencil, then a few simple
brush strokes, and here are
two donkey riders.

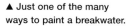

◄ The sky and sea were
painted very simply.

▼ Don't overlook subjects
like this. They make very
interesting paintings.

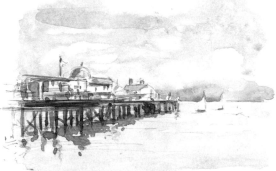

MUST KNOW

Have a sketch

When sitting on the beach, always have your 2B pencil and sketchbook at the
ready and just look around you for a suitable subject to draw. Anything from a
pebble to a group of bathers may take your fancy. Just have a go and sketch. Do
not forget that bathers or sea birds will move, but there will be plenty more for
you to draw. You can always try sketching some people who are asleep in
deckchairs – at least they will not move!

EXERCISE Paint a beach scene

This scene is painted from a rather unusual viewpoint, looking down on it from the top of the cliff. The breakwaters are a long way down and look quite small. The broken gate is close up which helps give the impression of distance. The shadows help to hold the whole painting together.

The palette

| French Ultramarine | Alizarin Crimson | Hooker's Green Dark | Yellow Ochre |

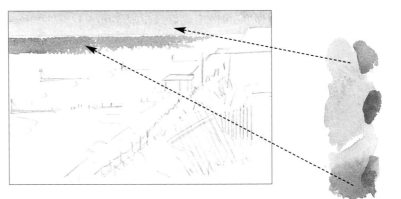

❶ Draw the scene with your 2B pencil. Paint the sky using your large brush, leaving a white horizontal line below it. Start painting in the sea using the dry-brush technique.

French Ultramarine
+ Alizarin Crimson
+ Hooker's Green Dark

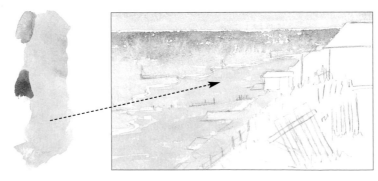

Yellow Ochre
+ Alizarin Crimson

❷ Continue painting the sea, adding more water as you work down. Next, paint the sand, leaving white paper for the hut.

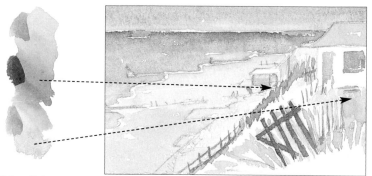

Yellow Ochre
+ Alizarin Crimson
+ Hooker's Green Dark

❸ Using your small brush, paint the pink roof, hut and grasses, then paint in the green grass. When dry, paint the windows on the building and the gate in the foreground.

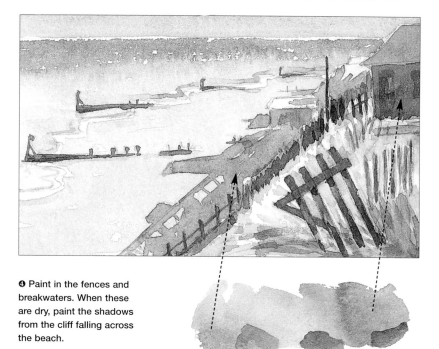

❹ Paint in the fences and breakwaters. When these are dry, paint the shadows from the cliff falling across the beach.

Yellow Ochre + Alizarin Crimson
+ French Ultramarine

▶ People on the beach

Seeing people enjoying themselves on the beach – children making sandcastles, people swimming in the sea, grandparents watching – will makes you feel that you must capture all these wonderful scenes. With the help of these exercises, you will soon be able to include people in your watercolour sketches.

Family holiday

This was painted from some pencil sketches made on the beach. The grandparents and the children are waving to the parents in the sea. The sea and the figures in the sea have been kept very simple. The most important element in the painting is the group in the foreground.

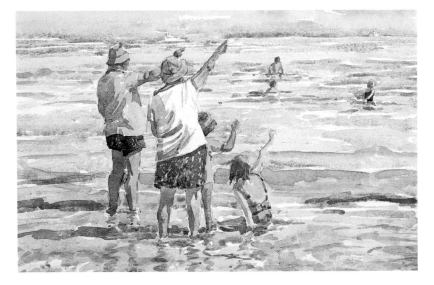

▲ The sea was painted very simply, with the colours changing as I worked down and around the figures with horizontal brush strokes, wet-on-wet. When dry, the figures were painted, and, finally, the shadows on the people and the sea were painted in.

MUST KNOW

Painting the sea
Always mix the colours you need before you start painting. Use a large brush filled with paint and plenty of water. Remember to leave white paper for any white-capped waves.

Placing people on the beach

When painting people on a beach, look for the horizon (this is your eye level). If the beach is level, the horizon will cross the people in the same place on their bodies (see below). Naturally people are different sizes, and the beach isn't always level, but this gives you something to work with.

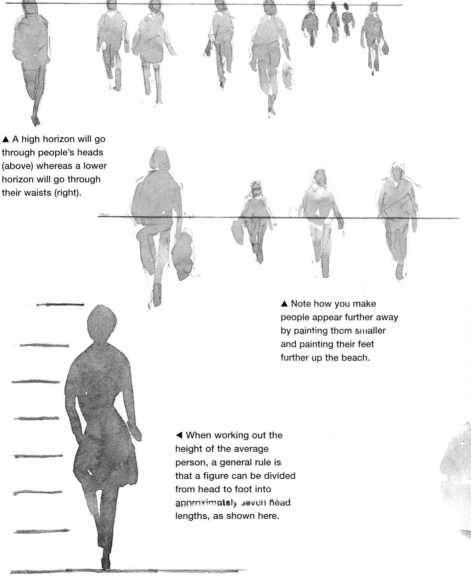

▲ A high horizon will go through people's heads (above) whereas a lower horizon will go through their waists (right).

▲ Note how you make people appear further away by painting them smaller and painting their feet further up the beach.

◄ When working out the height of the average person, a general rule is that a figure can be divided from head to foot into approximately seven head lengths, as shown here.

Girl playing

Children come in all shapes and sizes and don't stay still for a minute, making them difficult to paint, so practise painting them from photographs. This girl is nearly all in shadow, and you can almost feel the sun on her.

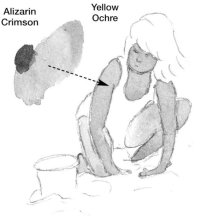

Alizarin Crimson

Yellow Ochre

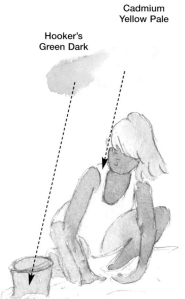

Hooker's Green Dark

Cadmium Yellow Pale

❶ Draw the girl with your 2B pencil. Paint her flesh with a small brush. Add more water to the top of the inside legs to make them paler.

❷ Let this dry, and then paint the hair, swimsuit and bucket, and let it dry again.

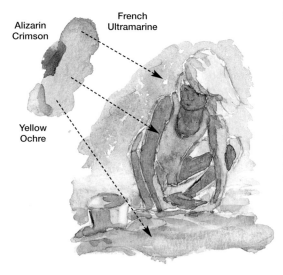

Alizarin Crimson

French Ultramarine

Yellow Ochre

❸ On the background, paint a wash using directional brush strokes. When dry, paint over the girl's body with a wash of shadow colour, leaving sunlit areas.

Group on the beach

You will see groups and couples walking on the beach. You don't want to put a lot of detail in them, as they are usually part of the scene and not the main subject. Too much detail would make them 'jump out' of the picture.

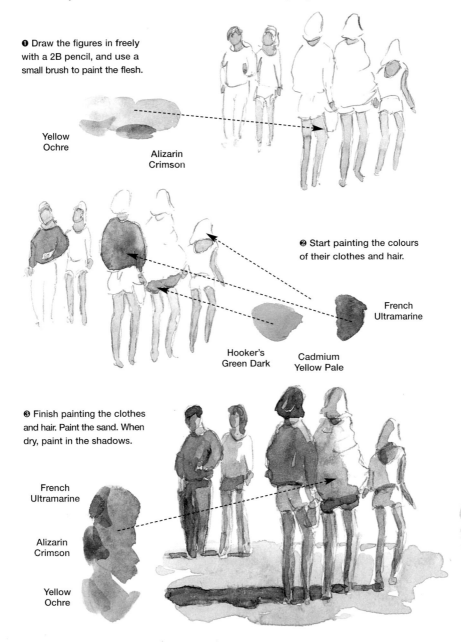

❶ Draw the figures in freely with a 2B pencil, and use a small brush to paint the flesh.

Yellow Ochre

Alizarin Crimson

❷ Start painting the colours of their clothes and hair.

French Ultramarine

Hooker's Green Dark

Cadmium Yellow Pale

❸ Finish painting the clothes and hair. Paint the sand. When dry, paint in the shadows.

French Ultramarine

Alizarin Crimson

Yellow Ochre

Sketching people on the beach

Sketching people is like sketching animals and birds. They never stay still.
As you can see from these sketches, you have to work quickly, and even
then some will have gone before you get any further than a few pencil
lines. Don't panic! Be patient, keep drawing and you will succeed. Start by
copying my sketches, and also use photographs; this is an acceptable
way to practise and will give you confidence when you go out to sketch.

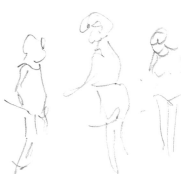

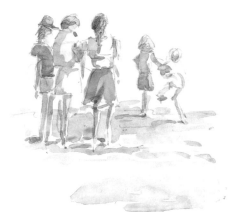

▲ This is as far as I got
before they moved!

▲ I was lucky this time;
these figures stayed still
long enough.

▼ The cast shadows from
the children help to anchor
them on the beach.

▲ You don't need more
detail than this: keep it
simple.

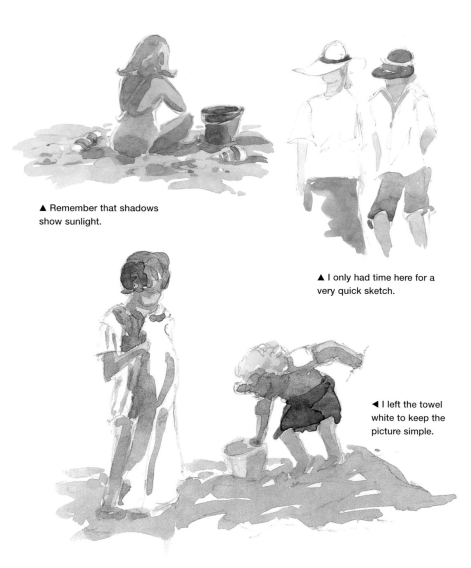

▲ Remember that shadows show sunlight.

▲ I only had time here for a very quick sketch.

◄ I left the towel white to keep the picture simple.

MUST KNOW

Working from photographs or television

As you have learned, people on the beach move so why not take your camera with you to the seashore and then you can practise painting at home, working from photographs. You can also sketch from the television by playing 'slow motion' or still frames. As you gain confidence, sketch them at normal speed on the TV and then from real life on the beach. Drawing anything that moves takes plenty of practice, so keep at it and enjoy it.

Boats

Some artists worry that painting boats will be difficult, believing them to be too technical, but if you observe them carefully and sketch what you see, they are easy. Study a boat, how it sits in the water, and where all the details go. Don't worry, your boat doesn't need to be seaworthy!

Yacht race

This was painted quickly and freely. The dark cloudy sky and dark water contrast with the white sails of the yachts and their reflections. The sails and some of the boats were left white to create a more dramatic effect.

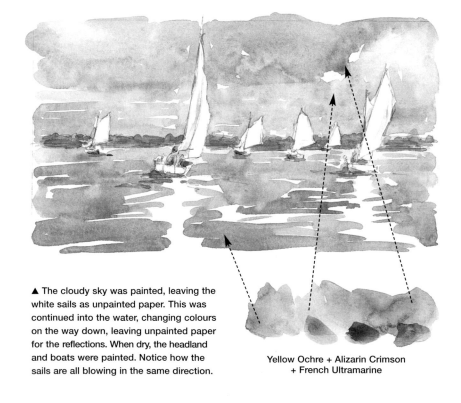

▲ The cloudy sky was painted, leaving the white sails as unpainted paper. This was continued into the water, changing colours on the way down, leaving unpainted paper for the reflections. When dry, the headland and boats were painted. Notice how the sails are all blowing in the same direction.

Yellow Ochre + Alizarin Crimson
+ French Ultramarine

PAINTING THE SEASHORE

122

Rowing boat

This rowing boat looks relatively simple, but you will still need to study its shape to make it sit realistically either in the water, or on the sand. If you copy this one carefully it will help you when you paint one on the beach.

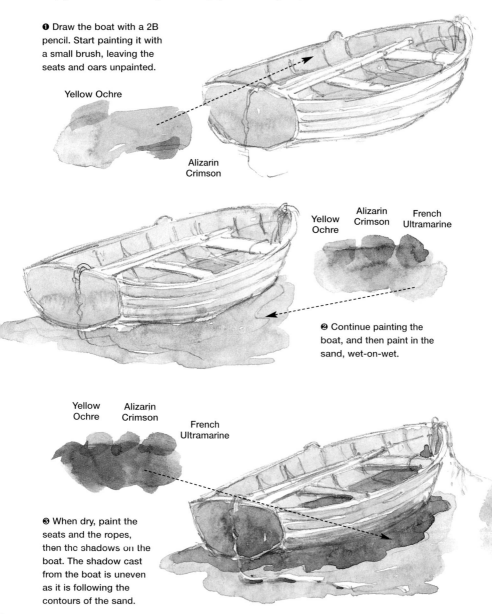

❶ Draw the boat with a 2B pencil. Start painting it with a small brush, leaving the seats and oars unpainted.

Yellow Ochre

Alizarin Crimson

Yellow Ochre   Alizarin Crimson   French Ultramarine

❷ Continue painting the boat, and then paint in the sand, wet-on-wet.

Yellow Ochre   Alizarin Crimson

French Ultramarine

❸ When dry, paint the seats and the ropes, then the shadows on the boat. The shadow cast from the boat is uneven as it is following the contours of the sand.

Sketching boats

Sketching helps to gather information for paintings, gives you memories to keep, or can be done just for the pleasure of it. Sketches can be paintings in their own right but are not usually very detailed. If you are doing a large sketch of boats, then use your rigger brush for the rigging, but if you are sketching on a small scale you may prefer to use your 2B pencil.

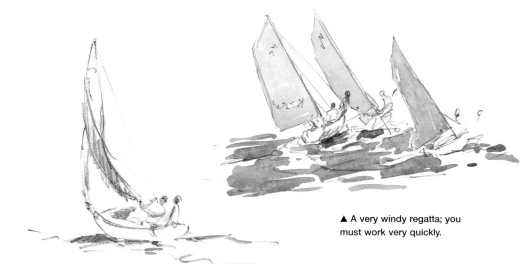

▲ A very windy regatta; you must work very quickly.

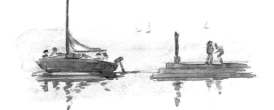

◀ Remember these sketches are very useful for information, even the silhouettes on the left.

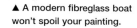

▲ A modern fibreglass boat won't spoil your painting.

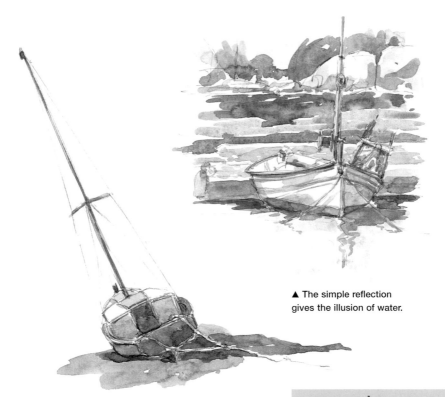

▲ The simple reflection gives the illusion of water.

▲ Notice how the rigging lines were left as pencil.

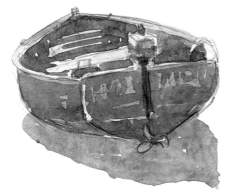

▲ The shadow from this rowing boat helps to sit it on the beach.

want to know more?

Take it to the next level...

Go to ...
► **Creating distance** – page 44
► **Water** – page 50
► **People in landscape** – page 62

Other sources
► **Photographs**
   useful sources of reference
► **Art shows**
   look out for local or national events
► **Internet**
   interactive CD-ROMs
► **Painting holidays**
   expand your horizons with other artists
► **Publications**
   visit www.collins.co.uk for Collins art books

paintng

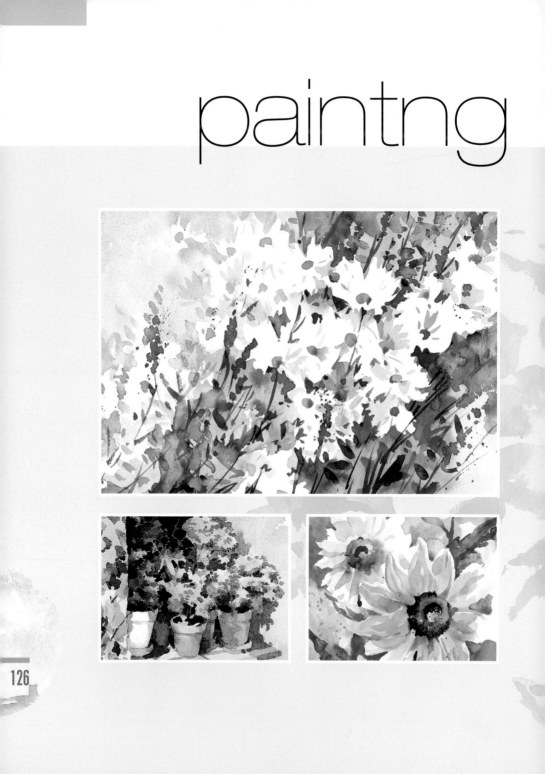

flowers

Flowers are a joy to paint; their infinite variety in shape and colour is an endless source of inspiration and challenge. Observation really is the key to revealing nature's secrets. The time that you spend looking at flowers will pay dividends in your painting, as you find that you develop an understanding of how the shapes and colours relate to one another.

Using your brush

Painting in watercolour is all about learning to control your brush. When painting flowers, a variety of marks can be made with a round brush that comes to a tip.

▶ Drawing with the brush

Your brush is a flexible tool and you can make different marks simply by varying the pressure you apply and the brush you use. All these marks were made by single strokes of a No. 8 brush.

▼ Two colours in the brush

Load the brush with two colours, one darker than the other, then press down on the paper using one brush stroke until you see both colours flowing out into the shape.

▲ Leaves in one stroke

The large leaf shape was painted with a single stroke of the brush starting at the tip, then working down the left-hand side and up the right-hand side, finishing back at the tip.

▼ Dry brush

Minimize the amount of liquid in your brush and drag it across the paper so that the pigment hits and misses the paper. This produces a sparkling effect and is very useful for creating texture.

▶ Soft edges

These can be created in two ways: you can either use water to form a shape and then add the paint, or you can paint the colour in and then add water to soften the edge. This technique is most helpful in producing three-dimensional form.

▶ Splashing and spattering

Load your brush with paint and whilst holding it over your dry or wet painting, tap with your index finger on the handle of the brush. This is very useful for adding random markings and texture.

Watercolour brushes

The best, and most expensive, brushes are made from sable; they have a long life, are ideal for holding a lot of liquid and encourage a delicacy of approach. Synthetic brushes have a lot of spring and tend to be easier to control, but they do not hold much liquid and their ability to come to a point is not long lasting. A good compromise is to use brushes that are made from a synthetic/sable mix.

▶ Flower shapes

The underlying shapes of flowers can help you to understand their structure. Recognizing and reproducing these shapes is all important to the confidence and simplicity of your finished work. This section shows you how to interpret the basic underlying shapes. All these exercises are worked using a No. 8 round brush. Have fun and invent some of your own.

Cup

This poppy is shaped like a cup. Thinking of it in this way will help you to simplify it when you are painting. You can try several times until you get a shape you are happy with.

❶ Starting with a pencil-drawn ellipse, draw in a triangular shape at the bottom to represent the underneath of the poppy, creating a cup shape. Clip out another triangle to represent the petals, add in the stem and finish with another ellipse for the centre.

Cadmium
Orange

Cadmium
Red

French
Ultramarine

❷ Take more clips out of the petals and paint in a variegated wash of Cadmium Orange and Cadmium Red. Paint a background of French Ultramarine. Add the stem (French Ultramarine with Cadmium Orange), and the dark centre (French Ultramarine with Cadmium Red).

Wheel

A clump of daisies always attracts the eye. Think of them as wheels with a hub and spokes, but without an outer rim. You can create the impression of the daisy with just a few marks.

❶ Paint the centre of the daisy using Indian Yellow and a touch of Cadmium Orange to add definition and depth.

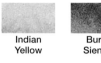

Indian Yellow	Burnt Sienna
Cadmium Orange	French Ultramarine

❷ Using the tip of the brush, paint Cadmium Orange for the centre and Burnt Sienna for the outer edge. Paint in some of the petals with French Ultramarine using single strokes of the brush. Try not to be too uniform in your approach and they will appear more natural.

❸ Continue in this way until your painting says 'daisy' to you. Don't add too much detail; leave some parts for the viewer's imagination.

Star

The star shape is seen in many forms in flowers. The star in the flower I've chosen doesn't need equal points; this gives it a more natural look.

Permanent
Mauve

Cadmium
Orange

❶ Start to map out the shape of the flower using Permanent Mauve. Keep the star shape in your mind and use the brush to create a loose interpretation.

Cadmium
Red

Yellow
Ochre

Coeruleum

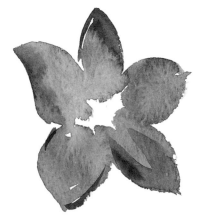

❷ Continue mapping out the shape of your flower, leaving white paper as a random shape in the centre.

❸ Use Cadmium Orange for the centre and then drop in a little Cadmium Red wet-into-wet. Using a stronger concentration of Permanent Mauve, mark the striations and divisions on the petals. With single brush strokes, add the stem and leaves, using some Yellow Ochre and Coeruleum.

Spiral

If you observe a rose developing from a bud to a full-blown flower you will see that it evolves in a spiral formation from the centre to the outside edge.

❶ Using Cadmium Red and Cadmium Orange, brush in the overall shape, allowing the colours to mix.

Cadmium
Red

Cadmium
Orange

French
Ultramarine

Indian
Yellow

Alizarin
Crimson

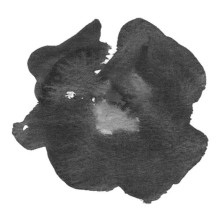

❷ Using a mix of French Ultramarine and Indian Yellow, paint a simple leaf shape with two strokes of the brush, leaving a white space along the centre to indicate its spine. With a mix of Alizarin Crimson and Cadmium Red, gently brush a few petal edges in, working from the centre outwards.

❸ Continue, adding more leaves, a stem, and defining more of the petals of the rose. Remember to vary the colour of the greens in the leaves and stem to make it look natural.

Trumpet

I like painting lilies because of their rich colours and diverse shapes. The initial cone shape opens out like a trumpet. Use the brush delicately when applying the paint.

Indian Yellow

Cadmium Orange

French Ultramarine

Permanent Mauve

Cadmium Red

❶ Start with a wash of Indian Yellow and Cadmium Orange, allowing the colours to mix on the paper to form the base of the lily. Flood into a triangular shape.

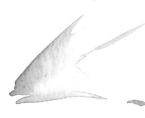

❷ Using a green made from Indian Yellow and French Ultramarine, flood a little into the base of the lily whilst it is still wet and continue down to form the stem. Start with blobs of a pale wash of Permanent Mauve to create the petals.

❸ Finish the blobs of Permanent Mauve to show the span of petals. Whilst still wet, paint in the stamens with Cadmium Red. Load the brush with Cadmium Orange and delicately, but directly, use the point to add in the striations on the petals. Add a little Cadmium Orange to the green to give a variety of tone in the stem.

PAINTING FLOWERS

Wing

I love the way irises moved by a gentle summer breeze appear to be flying. They have such a variety of colours and their petals resemble wings.

Coeruleum

Permanent Mauve

Cadmium Yellow

Cadmium Red

❶ Using Coeruleum, brush in the shape of the upper petals and then articulate the edges with some strokes of Permanent Mauve to create a sense of form.

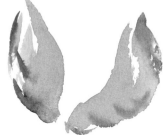

❷ Using more of the same colours, indicate the outer edges of the main petal and add a little more Permanent Mauve to the upper petals.

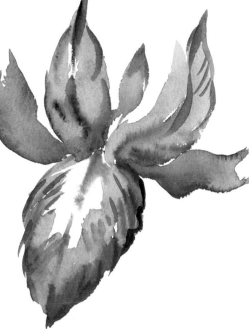

❸ Finish the petals by continuing in the same way, then paint the centre of the main petal in Cadmium Yellow, dropping in Cadmium Red whilst it is still wet.

Using colour

To reproduce the amazing colours of flowers, you need a basic understanding of colour theory. Your choice of colour combinations and their relative intensities is vital. For a bank of flowers of the same colour, it is exciting to explore the subtle differences of hue, whereas complementary colours, such as reds and greens, create drama and complexity.

Colour wheel

This colour wheel demonstrates the relationships between the colours.

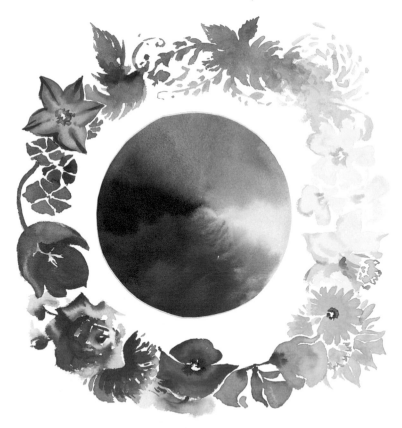

▲ Colours that are side by side, such as orange and yellow or blue and green, are called harmonizing.

Colours that are directly opposite one another, such as purple and yellow, are complementary.

Colours that are next door but one, such as green and orange or blue and yellow, are called contrasting.

Colour relationships

A thorough understanding of colour relationships will greatly increase your confidence when you are using different colours.

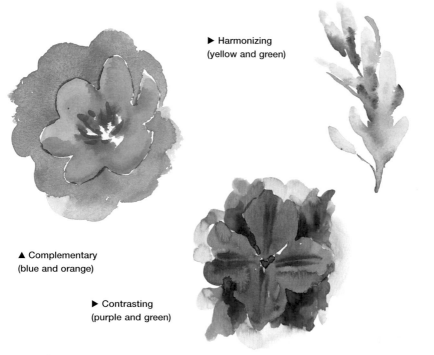

▶ Harmonizing
(yellow and green)

▲ Complementary
(blue and orange)

▶ Contrasting
(purple and green)

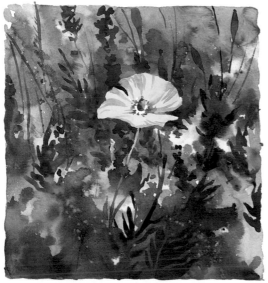

◀ Odd man out. In a field of yellow corn, a single poppy reigns supreme; it becomes the focus of attention. This is what I call the odd-man-out principle. You can use this colour device in many different ways to draw in the viewer's eye or encourage it to move throughout a painting. Even with dramatic colour this principle works, as you can see in this painting of a Welsh poppy.

Seasonal colours

It is possible to use similar colours but to create a different mood or atmosphere by using them in different proportions. For example, in the painting of spring, the yellows dominate and create a feeling of freshness, whereas in summer the warm blues and hot reds give a sense of heat.

Spring

Keep your colours fresh and clean and vary the yellows to create a natural effect.

Lemon
Yellow

Phthalo
Blue

Gamboge

Cadmium
Orange

Permanent
Mauve

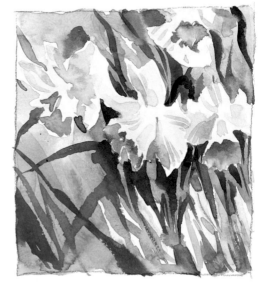

Summer

In order to create a summer feeling, use warm blues and reds applied softly.

Phthalo
Blue

Lemon
Yellow

Gamboge

Permanent
Rose

Alizarin
Crimson

Cobalt
Blue

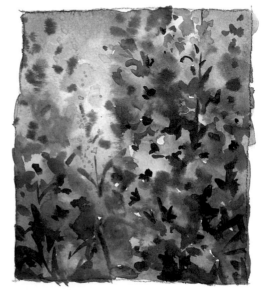

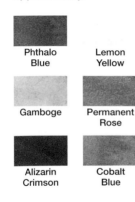

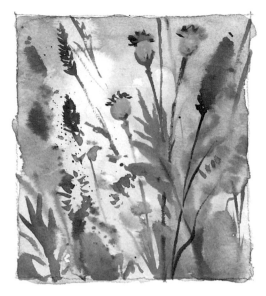

Autumn

A chance to practise your colour mixes so that the golden and burnt colours sing.

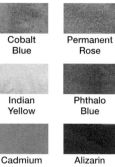

Cobalt Blue	Permanent Rose
Indian Yellow	Phthalo Blue
Cadmium Orange	Alizarin Crimson

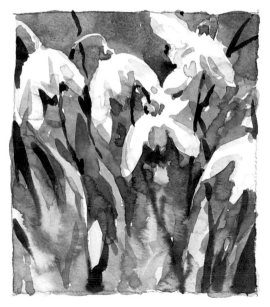

Winter

Cool colours and a large proportion of blue will help produce that wintry feeling.

Permanent Mauve	French Ultramarine
Phthalo Blue	Lemon Yellow
Alizarin Crimson	

White flowers

To give the whitest areas when painting in watercolours you leave the paper showing, so how much white you leave is crucial. The subtle colours you pick for shadows, or to mark out petals, need careful consideration. Try to see shadows and forms as abstract shapes; how they form the is the key.

▶ White rose

The amount of unpainted paper is at least 50 per cent of the total flower shape. I have used subtle colour variations in the folds and petals. Of course nothing in nature is completely white as it reflects colour from all around, so as you can see I have used a little of the background colour in the flower.

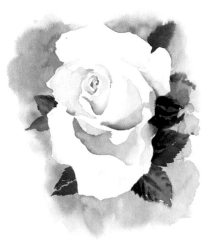

▼ White lilies

Here I started by painting the centres and allowed them to merge with the shadows of the petals. Then I painted the background, taking care to trap the shapes and help to bring the white areas forward. This is simple but effective.

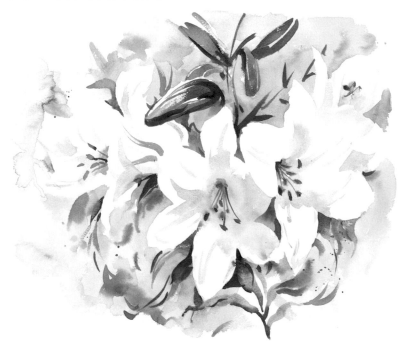

Mixing greens

Leaves and massed areas of foliage are necessary and important features in most flower paintings. The addition of a leaf or two should complement your flower shapes. A variety of different greens should be used. It is best to mix your own greens rather than use ready-mixed, and here I have given you examples of various mixed greens.

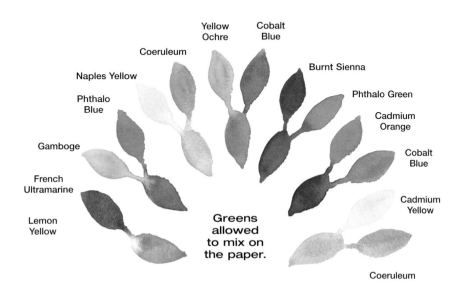

Yellow Ochre

Cobalt Blue

Coeruleum

Naples Yellow

Burnt Sienna

Phthalo Blue

Phthalo Green

Gamboge

Cadmium Orange

French Ultramarine

Cobalt Blue

Lemon Yellow

Cadmium Yellow

Greens allowed to mix on the paper.

Coeruleum

Useful dark greens, mixed thoroughly in the palette.

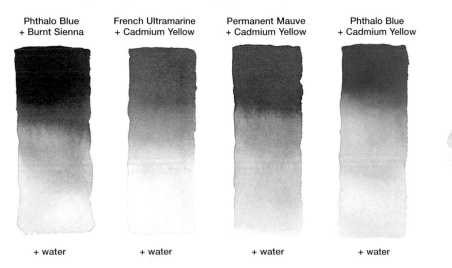

Phthalo Blue + Burnt Sienna	French Ultramarine + Cadmium Yellow	Permanent Mauve + Cadmium Yellow	Phthalo Blue + Cadmium Yellow
+ water	+ water	+ water	+ water

▶ Creating form

Without shadows your flowers will look flat. Light against dark
shows shape and form, and makes your flowers look three
dimensional. The wonderful thing about watercolour is that it is
transparent, making it an ideal medium for painting shadows,
as the original colours show through the shadow colour.

Peony

Colour and shadow should not oppose one another but work in unison;
remember that there are also colours evident in the shadows.

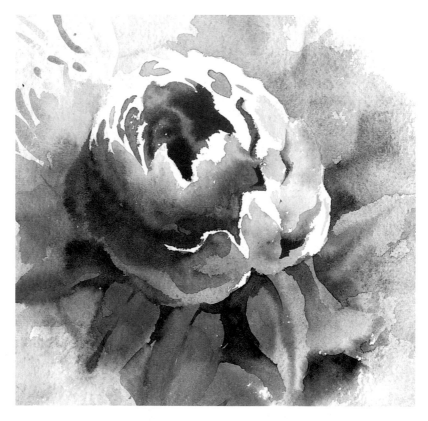

▲ The peony has a dark and a light side, an inside and an
outside. Establishing these areas will give your flower form. I
have used Cobalt Blue on the shadow side and left the white
of the paper to act as the light side. Dark Alizarin Crimson for
the inside helps to draw the eye.

Canary bird

This rose with its simple shape is a joy to paint. Large loose washes of
purple can be painted over areas of the painting when dry to create shadows.

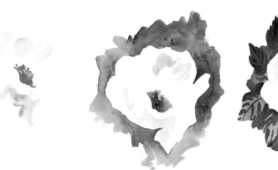

▲ This three-stage tonal study of the finished painting
below enables you to see the development of light
and dark without the complication of colour.

▶ Here I have used purple, the
complementary colour to yellow, for
the shadow areas over the flower. As
well as creating a sense of form this
also increases the effect of sunlight.
It is possible to use fairly loose
washes of paint once the light and
dark areas have been identified.

EXERCISE Paint a tulip

Using shadow is the main way to describe form in your paintings. In this
painting of a tulip I started with the shadow areas and, as you can see,
these form their own shape. Use your No. 8 brush for this exercise.

The palette

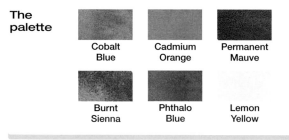

Cobalt
Blue

Cadmium
Orange

Permanent
Mauve

Burnt
Sienna

Phthalo
Blue

Lemon
Yellow

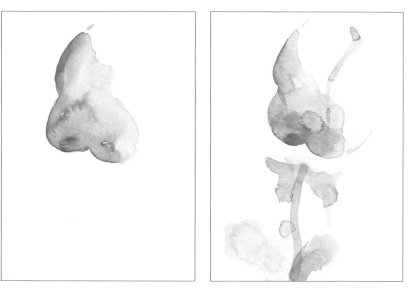

❶ Form the shadow area on the inside of the
tulip using Cobalt Blue and Permanent Mauve.
Create a smooth transition between the two
from dark to light. Whilst still wet, drop in
Cadmium Orange and Lemon Yellow.

❷ Put in two or three divisions for the petals
using Permanent Mauve. Then work pale
mixes of Phthalo Blue and Lemon Yellow for
the stem and background.

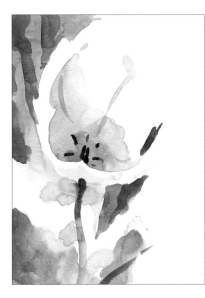

❸ In this stage you are promoting the light and dark in the background. Gradually show the outline shape of the tulip as you work. Put in the centre stamens with a mix of Burnt Sienna and Phthalo Blue.

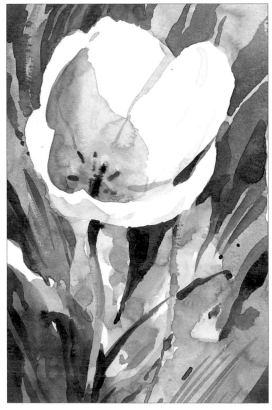

❹ Freely block in the rest of the background with variegated washes using mixes of Cobalt Blue, Lemon Yellow and Phthalo Blue. Add dark mixes of Permanent Mauve and Phthalo Blue for the negative shapes of the foliage. Finally, run in some graded Cobalt Blue to the original shadow to enhance the form.

Flower features

When painting flowers you need to consider their details, such as petals, buds, seed pods and leaves, as well as their texture, such as whether they are soft or prickly. Just look around you and you will find astonishing diversity. All the exercises in this section are painted with a No. 8 brush.

Petal

No two petals are the same, so this example will need to be varied when you put different petals together to paint a whole flower.

Coeruleum

Permanent Rose

Cadmium Orange

Cadmium Yellow

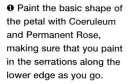

❶ Paint the basic shape of the petal with Coeruleum and Permanent Rose, making sure that you paint in the serrations along the lower edge as you go.

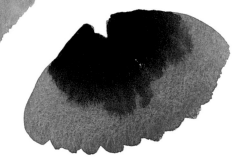

❷ A darker concentration of your previous mix of purple wet-into-wet is used for the darker pattern; feed it in with the tip of your brush.

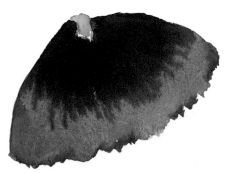

❸ Paint in the striations and darken the edge of the petal. Drop in a little Cadmium Orange mixed with Cadmium Yellow to indicate the centre.

Bud

All flowers have buds of different shapes, sizes and colours. Here I have chosen a rose bud for you to try. Study buds carefully and paint as many different types as you can so that you have them for reference when you are painting more complex pictures later.

Permanent
Rose

Alizarin
Crimson

Coeruleum

Cadmium
Yellow

❶ Load your brush with Permanent Rose and use it to create the overall shape, remembering to make use of the white of the paper.

❷ Drop in Alizarin Crimson to create depth. Paint the green of the sepals with a mix of Coeruleum and Cadmium Yellow.

❸ Add a little Permanent Rose to the green to make it darker and paint in the dark green accents. Use Alizarin Crimson to define the central petals.

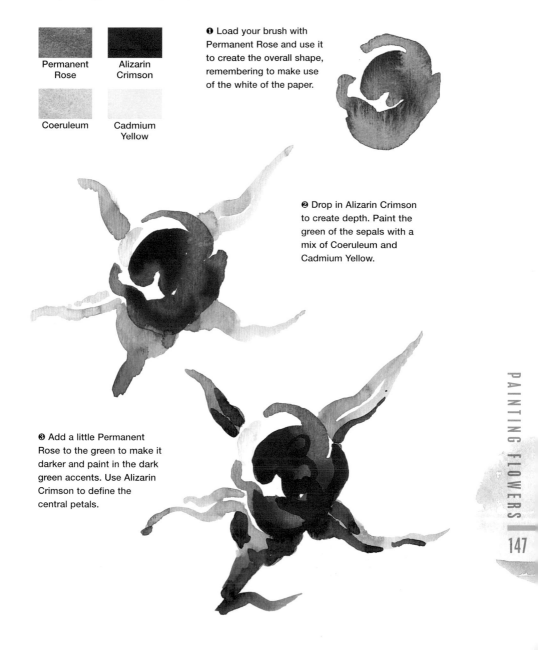

Seed pod

There is tremendous variety in the different seed pods and heads of flowers. Although the shapes can look complex it is possible to simplify them. Have a go at this simple poppy seed pod.

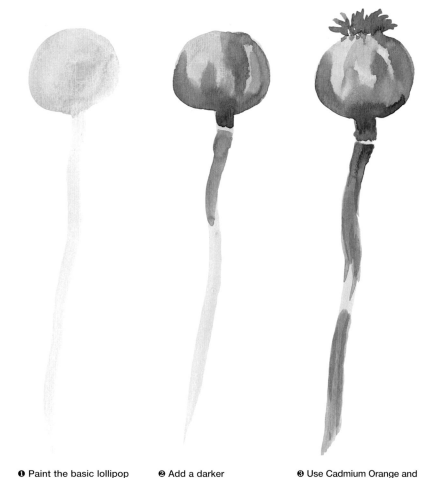

❶ Paint the basic lollipop shape in with Coeruleum. Add the stem with a single stroke of the brush.

❷ Add a darker concentration of Coeruleum with a touch of Cadmium Yellow whilst still wet to create the form.

❸ Use Cadmium Orange and a touch of Burnt Sienna to paint the spiky top of the seed pod and flood a little into the base of the pod. Add darker definition to the stem.

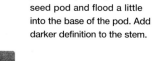

Coeruleum   Cadmium Yellow   Cadmium Orange   Burnt Sienna

Leaf

Whether you live in the town or country you are surrounded by different types of leaves. Try to handle the shapes as simply as possible. This whole exercise is painted quickly wet-into-wet (see page 17).

❶ Paint in a basic leaf shape with simple brush strokes using Cadmium Yellow. Drop in Cobalt Blue and allow to mix.

❷ Add a little Burnt Sienna to articulate the serrated edge on the left of the leaf.

❸ Continue with Burnt Sienna on the right-hand side and paint in the veins and stem of the leaf.

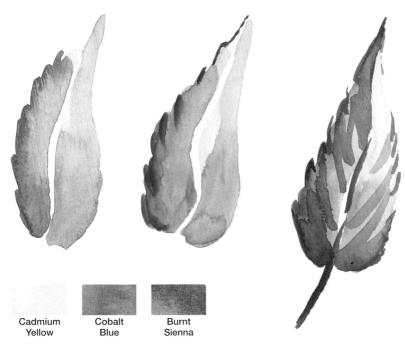

Cadmium Yellow

Cobalt Blue

Burnt Sienna

MUST KNOW

Painting leaves

When painting a new leaf, study it carefully and determine the overall shape. Then pay attention to the divisions and colour variations. Even when leaves are from the same plant there is diversity, so remember this when you are painting, and don't paint them all the same. Be aware that what you are aiming for is an impression of a leaf, or group of leaves, not a botanical illustration.

EXERCISE Paint an oriental poppy

Oriental poppies have a lovely simple shape with easily recognizable features. I have taken a simple view to include the features both inside and outside the flower. Once you get the basic elements in place you can have a great deal of fun with the rest.

The palette

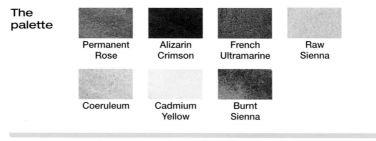

Permanent Rose	Alizarin Crimson	French Ultramarine	Raw Sienna

Coeruleum	Cadmium Yellow	Burnt Sienna

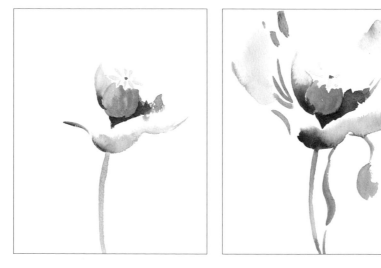

❶ Place a dot of green (Coeruleum and Raw Sienna) with the tip of a No. 10 brush. Add a wheel of Cadmium Yellow spokes. Paint the green ball of the seed head, adding extra Coeruleum to the wash. A single brush stroke provides the stem. Add a wash of Permanent Rose around the seed head and drop in Alizarin Crimson to form a V-shape in the centre and a touch beneath the lower petal.

❷ Extend the washes of Permanent Rose, dropping in Alizarin Crimson to form the petals. Try to use single strokes of the brush as this gives a clean, transparent effect. With your green mix add the bud. These tend to hang over whereas seed heads stand up straight. Always try to reflect nature in your flower paintings.

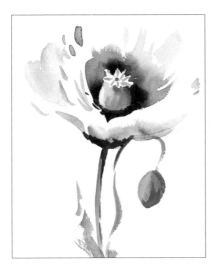

❸ To create more form begin to bring in darker tones both inside and out. Use French Ultramarine with Alizarin Crimson around the centre and to the base of the poppy, plus a stroke of French Ultramarine at the top of the stem where a shadow would be cast. Complete the bud with some cool mixes of Coeruleum and Raw Sienna, and begin a leaf at the base with a few strokes of the brush.

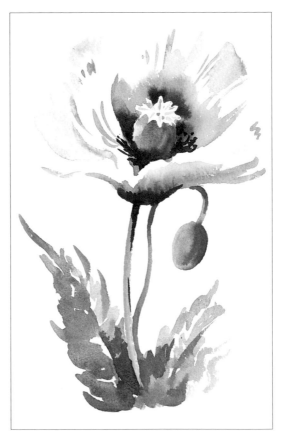

❹ Extend and vary the leaves at the base with colours ranging from French Ultramarine to almost pure Raw Sienna. This helps to give the leaves their bluish quality. Keep an open quality to your brushwork and do not do too much blending. Add in the dark accents to the poppy with a mix of Burnt Sienna and French Ultramarine. Add some creases and striations to the petals until the whole shape forms.

Foliage

Foliage is often only considered as an afterthought in a flower painting, but it should be an integral part of the whole painting. Leaf shapes and massed areas of foliage can be exciting and diverse, and they add life and depth to your paintings. This section suggests a few different ways you can explore painting leaves and foliage.

Leaves

Painting every leaf in full detail and with equal attention can make your painting look fussy and can detract from your flower forms. Remember that the angles of leaves and stems are important to the overall design and should not be overworked. Large sweeps of the brush can do a lot to create the impression of leaves, so keep details such as veins to a minimum.

▲ The leaves of this French rose were painted with single strokes of a brush loaded with two different colours. The way they are placed echoes nature and also creates a sense of movement. I have taken some of the colour from the rose and repeated it in the leaves to tie them together.

Leaf shapes

These leaves range from blue to almost brown. It is very important to vary the colours, sizes, shapes and ways of rendering your leaves. Ask yourself what the basic colours are, then explore as many as you can.

▼ All these leaves are from different flowers; see how the shapes, colours and textures change.

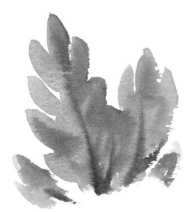

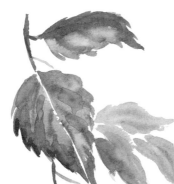

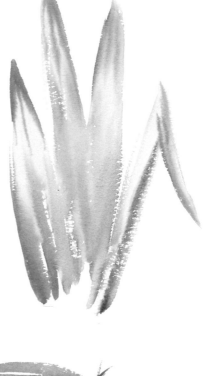

Massed foliage

If you start with amorphous shapes you can add definition later on. Keep an eye on the overall effect. Cover all the large areas first and then return to add details; this will help to keep your washes fresh and flowing.

◀ Large areas of foliage can be painted in numerous ways. It is important to see the broader shape of the mass first, and show the specific shapes at the edges. These three examples show different types of foliage. It can be helpful to think of them as simple silhouettes.

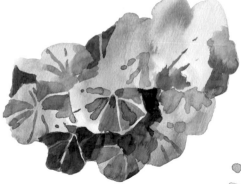

▲ Nasturtium leaves

This is what I call a 'reversing out' procedure. I painted in the general colours of the leaves as a variegated wash and then used the darker leaves to 'reverse out' the lighter ones. Pay attention to the negative areas.

► Flower border

When your flowers are seen as part of a herbaceous border, 75 per cent of the view can be of foliage. Here I have used bluer washes in the background and warmer greens in the foreground. The dark negative areas tie together both background and foreground.

MUST KNOW

Painting massed foliage

A simple way to approach massed foliage is to start painting from the general to the particular, i.e. paint in the overall shape first and then add in the subdivisions and details. It is important to remember only to add those details that are necessary. If you paint the details first, you will find yourself trying to protect them and this will make the whole exercise far more difficult and can even result in an overall lack of cohesion.

Composition

Composition or design is the term applied to how your painting is arranged, or, in this case, where you place your flowers within the space. It refers to the elements you place within the format. The format is the window area that you are painting on. Many formats are possible, but most often the format is rectangular or square and either horizontal or vertical.

Movement

Composition can create a sense of movement and can give you confidence with the placement of your flower shapes and foliage. Its main aim is to provide you with more freedom of execution.

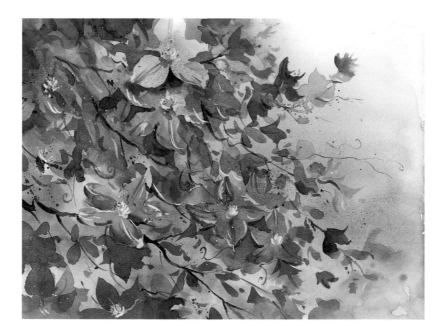

▲ In this painting of purple clematis I chose a horizontal format and took a diagonal line of movement on which I pivoted my flower shapes and foliage. Making this decision at the beginning gave me the opportunity for greater freedom of expression.

Thumbnail sketches

The benefit of a simple thumbnail sketch is that it gives you a plan that you can follow. Here are some simple ones for you to practise.

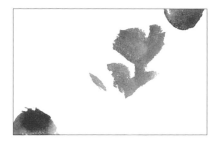

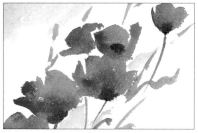

▲ Diagonal
Start by placing the main shapes of the flower heads in a diagonal composition and then build the painting outwards from there.

▲ Off-centre
Place the buds and foliage slightly left of centre and add in the flowers to achieve an off-centre composition and again continue outwards. Here I dropped in a simple blue wash to throw the pale flowers forwards.

Focal point

As well as a strong composition, you will also need a focal point. This is the area of interest in a painting that draws the viewer's eye. A useful tip is to place the focal point at an unequal distance from all four sides of the painting.

Here you can see a thumbnail sketch and a more finished painting showing a triangular composition which helps to lead your eye to the focal point, the main daisy.

Relative sizes

It is very important to vary the relative sizes of the flowers within your painting in order to create interest. For example, it is useful to include large, medium and small shapes; you may find it helpful to remember this as the 'daddy, mummy, baby' principle.

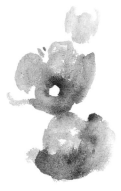 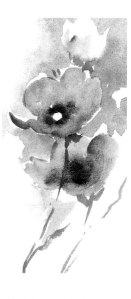 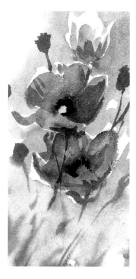

❶ With your No. 8 brush, paint in the overall shape of three pink oriental poppies using Alizarin Crimson, and, whilst still wet, brush in a little Permanent Mauve. Remember the 'daddy, mummy, baby' principle.

❷ Using a green made from Coeruleum mixed with a little Yellow Ochre, add in the cups beneath the flowers, and the stems. With the same colours, but predominantly Coeruleum, start to add in a simple wash background.

❸ Add in a few more stems and poppy heads with a darker mix of your green and then complete this simple painting by finishing the background wash using a variety of the colours already used in the painting.

Alizarin
Crimson

Permanent
Mauve

Coeruleum

Yellow
Ochre

EXERCISE Paint carnations

In this study of carnations, keep the basic shapes of each flower simple. Concentrate more on the design in the initial stages, using the background colours to throw the lighter forms forward in the final stage.

The palette

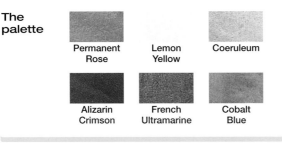

| Permanent Rose | Lemon Yellow | Coeruleum |
| Alizarin Crimson | French Ultramarine | Cobalt Blue |

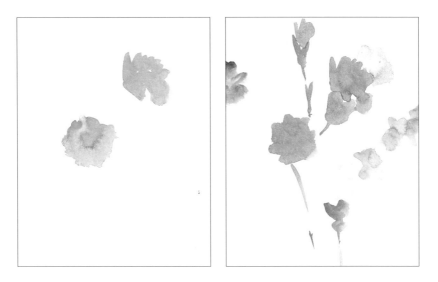

❶ Start by placing three initial shapes attractively within the picture space. These can be done with flat blobs of colour using Permanent Rose and Lemon Yellow, and your No. 8 brush.

❷ Flesh out more of the design by working rapidly towards the edges of the paper; this will give you a quick grasp of the overall design. Use Coeruleum and Lemon Yellow to create the greens.

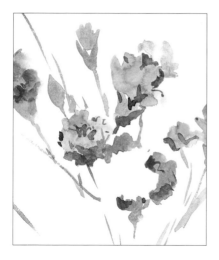

❸ Add in some darks at this stage to create some form on the flowers with washes of Alizarin Crimson; use French Ultramarine for the foliage. Keep adding stems as you feel the design growing.

❹ When you feel you have enough flower heads placed, start adding background washes around them with Cobalt Blue, Lemon Yellow and Permanent Rose in variegated form. Finally, add some wet-into-wet carnations to the bottom left-hand side of the painting.

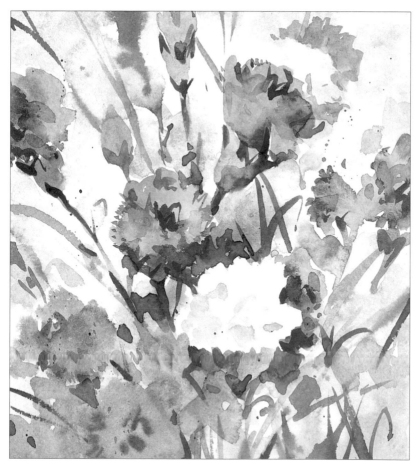

Garden flowers

You will find inspiration in any garden border; shapes and colours are always amassed to give the artist a wealth of riches to draw upon. I grow the flowers that I like to paint in my garden. There are also many gardens that are open to the public where you are often welcome to paint.

Pansy

Pansies have plenty of movement in them as well as rich colours and texture. Their light and dark patterns are an added bonus for an artist.

❶ Take your No. 8 brush and place Cadmium Red and Cadmium Yellow in the centre of the paper, working out with a skirt of purple made from Cadmium Red andFrench Ultramarine. Begin to indicate the petals with small washes of Naples Yellow, and allow to dry.

❷ Paint a wash in the negative areas of the background. The greens are a free mix of Cadmium Yellow, Coeruleum, French Ultramarine and Cadmium Orange. Place washes of Permanent Mauve for the shadow areas on the flower. Strengthen the dark centre.

Cadmium Red	Cadmium Yellow
French Ultramarine	Naples Yellow
Coeruleum	Cadmium Orange
Permanent Mauve	

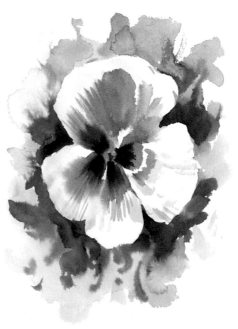

Daisy

A common mistake when painting daisies in watercolour is not to leave enough white paper showing for the petals. This exercise avoids this error by painting in the background last of all.

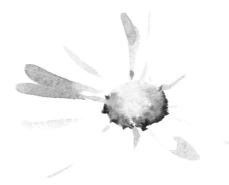

❶ Paint in the central ellipse with your No. 8 brush and dilutions of Gamboge, Cadmium Orange and Burnt Sienna. Allow to mix on the paper as much as possible.

❷ Indicate a few of the shadows on the petals with an even mix of Coeruleum and Permanent Rose. Take care not to make them all the same. Strengthen the Burnt Sienna around the edge of the centre.

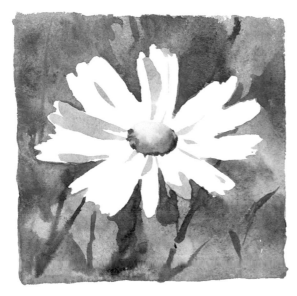

Gamboge	Cadmium Orange
Burnt Sienna	Coeruleum
Permanent Rose	Cadmium Yellow
French Ultramarine	

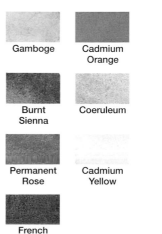

❸ Mix washes of Cadmium Yellow, French Ultramarine and Coeruleum in various combinations before you start. Paint in a variegated wash, dropping in darks with French Ultramarine, and being careful to paint around the petals.

Rose

I love painting roses and for me they are the most complete flower. I feel that they represent a wholeness of form and colour, making them a sheer joy to paint for any flower artist.

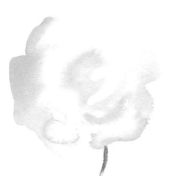

Cadmium Red	Indian Yellow	Burnt Sienna

Coeruleum	Cobalt Blue

❶ Using your No. 14 brush, put down a wash of Indian Yellow to form the centre and soften the edges with some water and a little Cadmium Red to create the outer petals. Let it dry.

❷ Paint a loose wash of Cobalt Blue to form the outer shape. Whilst still damp, start to add leaves made from mixes of Cobalt Blue and Indian Yellow. Develop the rose with your No. 8 brush using Indian Yellow and Cadmium Red.

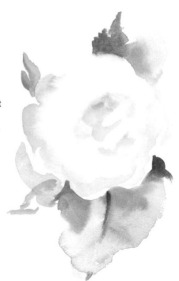

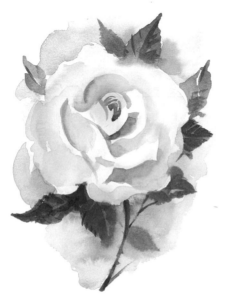

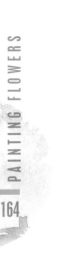

❸ Work from the centre of the rose outwards with smaller shapes at first using more concentrated colour to form the petals. Soften the edges with water as you go along. Put a wash of Cobalt Blue around the outside and then add some leaves and details of veining.

Camellia

The exotic-looking camellia belongs to a group of plants which includes the tea plant. The dark green glossy leaves create a dynamic contrast with the delicate petals, making it very enjoyable to paint.

❶ Using your No. 8 brush, paint the centre with Cadmium Orange and Lemon Yellow. Start some of the divisions on the petals with a mix of Permanent Rose and French Ultramarine.

❷ Add further divisions of petals, then establish the outside shape with foliage using varying mixes of Phthalo Blue, Cadmium Red and Lemon Yellow.

Cadmium Orange

Lemon Yellow

Permanent Rose

French Ultramarine

Phthalo Blue

Cadmium Red

Indian Yellow

Permanent Mauve

Burnt Sienna

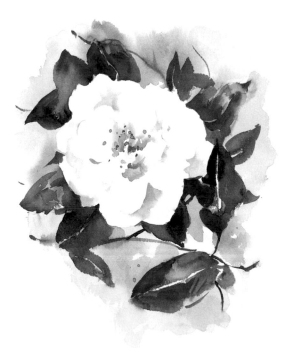

❸ Finish articulating the leaves, then add further details to the petals. Drop in a variegated background wash using Indian Yellow, Cadmium Red and Permanent Mauve. When dry, splash Cadmium Orange and Burnt Sienna across the centre to represent the seeds.

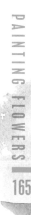

Delphiniums

Although delphiniums are complex, you should simplify their overall shapes when you paint them. Treat every flower initially as a blob of paint, adding any necessary detail at a later stage.

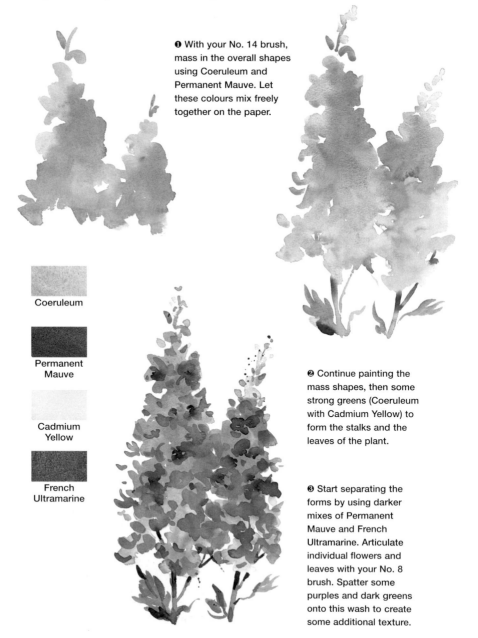

❶ With your No. 14 brush, mass in the overall shapes using Coeruleum and Permanent Mauve. Let these colours mix freely together on the paper.

Coeruleum

Permanent Mauve

Cadmium Yellow

French Ultramarine

❷ Continue painting the mass shapes, then some strong greens (Coeruleum with Cadmium Yellow) to form the stalks and the leaves of the plant.

❸ Start separating the forms by using darker mixes of Permanent Mauve and French Ultramarine. Articulate individual flowers and leaves with your No. 8 brush. Spatter some purples and dark greens onto this wash to create some additional texture.

Sunflowers

When you paint these sunflowers, use the exercise as a guide. Don't feel you need to follow it exactly, but try to create your own painting.

Lemon Yellow	Gamboge	Cadmium Orange	Permanent Mauve

French Ultramarine	Coeruleum	Cobalt Blue	Burnt Sienna

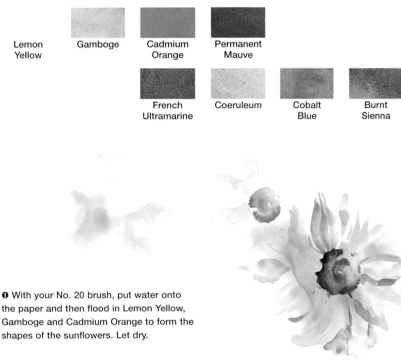

❶ With your No. 20 brush, put water onto the paper and then flood in Lemon Yellow, Gamboge and Cadmium Orange to form the shapes of the sunflowers. Let dry.

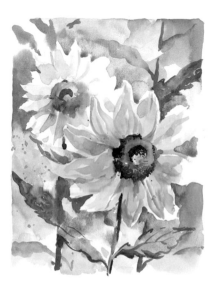

❷ Using your No. 8 brush, paint the flower centres with Cadmium Orange and Permanent Mauve. Use a mix of Cadmium Orange and Gamboge for the petals, leaving some of the yellow showing through. Blush in some green (French Ultramarine, Gamboge and Coeruleum).

❸ Use French Ultramarine and Lemon Yellow to paint the foliage in the negative spaces. Add Permanent Mauve to the background Paint leaves and stems with single brush strokes of two colours. A little Cobalt Blue adds depth to the foliage. Enhance the darks with Permanent Mauve and Burnt Sienna. Splash a dark mix of Lemon Yellow and French Ultramarine onto the foliage.

EXERCISE **Paint a garden border**

In this painting, the daisies rely on a technique that I call reversal, because you are painting around the subject and not the subject itself. It is useful to practise because it throws the subject into relief.

The palette

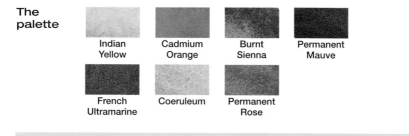

Indian Yellow   Cadmium Orange   Burnt Sienna   Permanent Mauve

French Ultramarine   Coeruleum   Permanent Rose

❶ Load your No. 6 brush with Cadmium Orange and place some of the centres of the daisies around the focal point of the picture. Don't crowd them too close together. Use Permanent Mauve for shadow areas, bringing out the suggestion of daisies straight away. Drop Burnt Sienna into a couple of yellow centres.

❷ With a wash of French Ultramarine and Coeruleum allowed to mix freely on the paper, paint in the background negative shape to bring out the main clump of daisies. Add a mix of Coeruleum and Indian Yellow to indicate some of the foliage. Add some darker blobs of Permanent Mauve for the lavender and a few more towards the bottom of the painting.

❸ Work on both the right-
and left-hand sides, taking
care to leave areas of white
paper. Daisies should start
appearing miraculously
from the apparently random
shapes. Use splashing to
create some lavender heads.

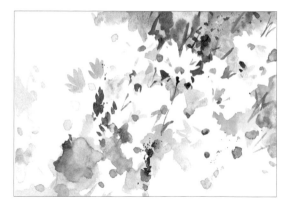

❹ Use a No. 10 brush to
wash in greens made from
varying mixes of Coeruleum,
French Ultramarine and
Indian Yellow. Try to
connect the greens across
the painting to ceate a
sense of harmony. Use the
tip of the brush for the
sweeping lines of stems and
leaves in single strokes and
the body of the brush for
larger wash areas.

❺ Add a wash of Coeruleum
to the top left and pull it
through the shadow areas
down towards the greens to
tie the background in to the
subject. Paint in more
lavender with the splashing
technique and add some
further shadows from a mix
of French Ultramarine and
Permanent Rose.

Wild flowers

Wild flowers are all around you, whether you live in the town or the country. They proliferate on roadsides as well as in neglected corners of the garden. Once you start to look you will notice them everywhere. A woodland filled with bluebells or a stray poppy is always a joy to paint.

Buttercups

Bright yellow buttercups with shiny petals are lovely to paint. This simple view of buttercups shows the beauty of loose handling and fresh colours.

❶ Take your No. 8 brush and Lemon Yellow and paint some buttercup shapes. They have five petals. Mix a fresh spring green using Coeruleum and Lemon Yellow and add the stems and leaves. Put in a touch of Burnt Sienna for extra coloration. Leave to dry.

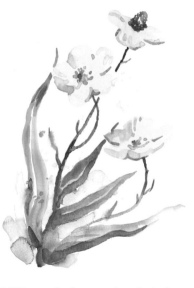

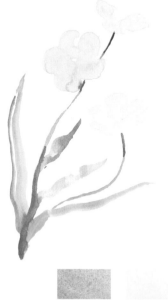

❷ With your fresh green mix, paint in the centre of the buttercups, adding a little French Ultramarine to the darker side. Using small stabs of a brush loaded with Cadmium Orange, paint into the green centres. Articulate the foliage.

Coeruleum

Lemon Yellow

Burnt Sienna

Cadmium Orange

French Ultramarine

Field poppy

The red field poppy is surely the king of wild flowers. This exercise gives you a chance to use all the reds against a background of purple and cool greens.

❶ Paint the basic poppy shape using Cadmium Red and Cadmium Orange. Use darker mixes of Permanent Rose and French Ultramarine for the centre and stem.

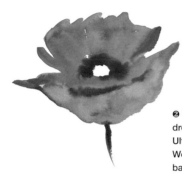

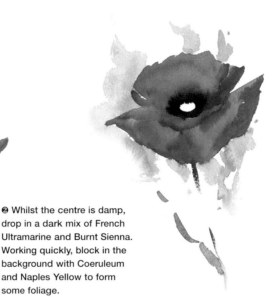

❷ Whilst the centre is damp, drop in a dark mix of French Ultramarine and Burnt Sienna. Working quickly, block in the background with Coeruleum and Naples Yellow to form some foliage.

Cadmium Red

Cadmium Orange

Permanent Rose

Burnt Sienna

French Ultramarine

Coeruleum

Naples Yellow

❸ Work the background details up using stronger mixes of greens and purples. Try to keep the background wet-into-wet as much as possible. Paint the striations and divisions on the petals of the poppy.

Bluebells

Bluebells are a delightful sight, emerging in wooded areas from late spring onwards. A few fine days should allow you to get outside to paint them.

❶ With your No. 8 brush use a mix of Cobalt Blue and Coeruleum to paint in some of the bell shapes.

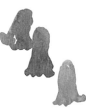

Cobalt
Blue

Coeruleum

Permanent
Rose

Cadmium
Yellow

Cadmium
Orange

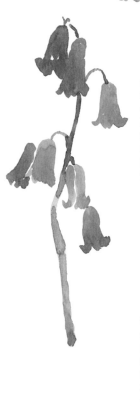

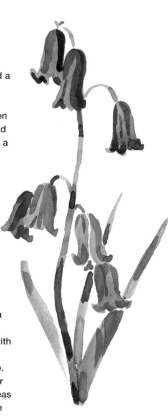

❷ Paint in more bells. Add a little Permanent Rose to vary the colour to purple. Paint the stem with a green mixed from Coeruleum and Cadmium Yellow. Blush in a little Cadmium Orange at the base of the stem.

❸ Enhance the darks for a more three-dimensional effect. Divide the petals with a stronger mix of Cobalt Blue and Permanent Rose. Use a stronger mix of your green to paint shadow areas to the stem and add some leaves. Ensure that they underlap the bells.

Forget-me-nots

Handle this spray of forget-me-nots simply and paint them straight onto the paper so there is nothing to interfere with the freshness of the colours.

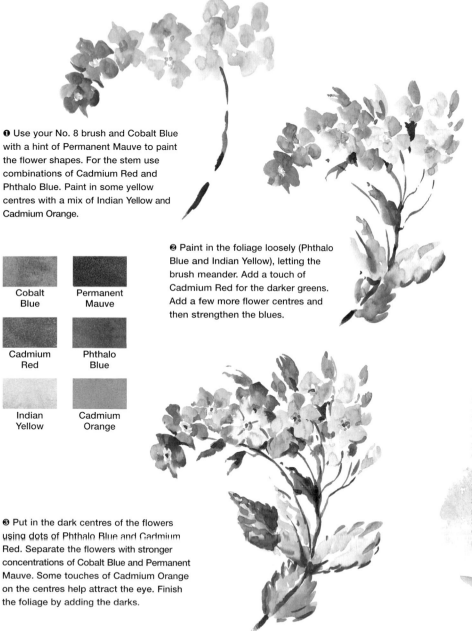

❶ Use your No. 8 brush and Cobalt Blue with a hint of Permanent Mauve to paint the flower shapes. For the stem use combinations of Cadmium Red and Phthalo Blue. Paint in some yellow centres with a mix of Indian Yellow and Cadmium Orange.

Cobalt Blue	Permanent Mauve
Cadmium Red	Phthalo Blue
Indian Yellow	Cadmium Orange

❷ Paint in the foliage loosely (Phthalo Blue and Indian Yellow), letting the brush meander. Add a touch of Cadmium Red for the darker greens. Add a few more flower centres and then strengthen the blues.

❸ Put in the dark centres of the flowers using dots of Phthalo Blue and Cadmium Red. Separate the flowers with stronger concentrations of Cobalt Blue and Permanent Mauve. Some touches of Cadmium Orange on the centres help attract the eye. Finish the foliage by adding the darks.

EXERCISE	Meadow

In a wild flower meadow, there is a myriad of flowers of unusual colours and shapes, ensuring that there is always something interesting for you to paint. Take your sketchbook out into the fields on a warm sunny day.

The palette

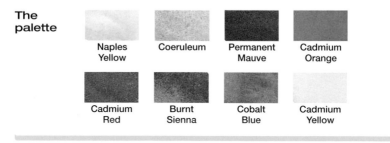

Naples Yellow	Coeruleum	Permanent Mauve	Cadmium Orange
Cadmium Red	Burnt Sienna	Cobalt Blue	Cadmium Yellow

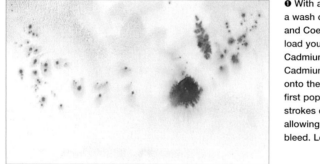

❶ With a No. 20 brush paint a wash of Naples Yellow and Coeruleum. Whilst wet load your No. 8 brush with Cadmium Orange and Cadmium Red and splash onto the paper. Start the first poppy with a few brush strokes of the same colours, allowing the colours to bleed. Let this dry.

❷ With Cadmium Red and Cadmium Orange, add definition to the first poppy and paint the petals of the two main poppies. Place dots of Cadmium Yellow and patches of Permanent Mauve randomly across the paper. Drop in the centre of the right-hand poppy (Permanent Mauve with a hint of Burnt Sienna). Let this dry.

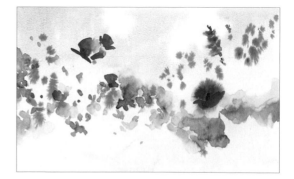

❸ Add foliage using green (Coeruleum and Cadmium Yellow, more blue than yellow). The darker green is Cobalt Blue and Cadmium Yellow. Add in the petals of the foreground poppy. Do not add too much detail to the daisies: place the yellow centres, then brush in the foliage around them to create some daisy shapes.

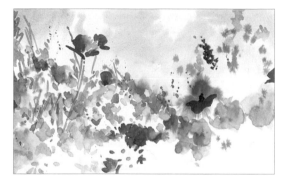

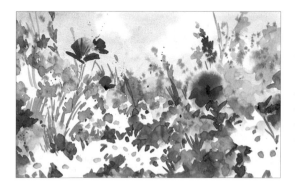

❹ Continue working the broader areas of the flowers and foliage. Remember to vary the colours you are using. Add a little Burnt Sienna to the Cadmium Yellow in the foreground on the right. Suggest the daisies bottom right in a similar way to those in the previous stage.

❺ Start adding a few details here and there, but do not add too many; you want to create the tangled effect of a wild flower meadow. Paint in a few more grasses with single strokes of the brush. Finally, use a bit of splashing with Cobalt Blue and Permanent Mauve to give the effect of extra flowers.

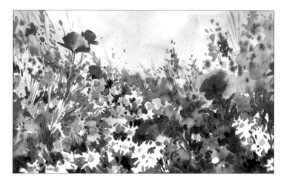

Backgrounds

How the background interacts with the subject of your painting is vitally important to the overall look, especially in flower painting. The background needs to be considered as an integral part of the painting process, not merely as an afterthought. In this section I will show you some different ways of approaching backgrounds in watercolour as an effective means of creating impact in your paintings.

Negative spaces

When you take a simple group of flowers, the important thing to note is the shape of the spaces between them; these are referred to as negative spaces and are an essential ingredient for painting backgrounds.

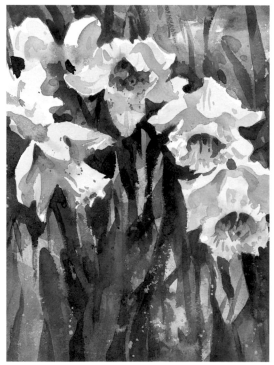

▶ In this painting of daffodils, lights and darks have been added to create drama. The negative spaces are complex but all the flower heads are a great deal lighter than the background tones.

MUST KNOW

Creating impact in your painting
Start off with a small division between two flowers – it will usually be triangular or diamond in shape – and then work outwards from there. This will help give your painting immediate impact and cast the flowers forward.

Flowers first

If your subject matter is lighter than the background, see the background as a negative shape and paint around the flower shapes. In this exercise it is easy to see the negative shapes of the background between the petals.

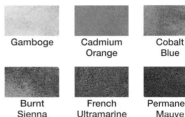

Gamboge	Cadmium Orange	Cobalt Blue
Burnt Sienna	French Ultramarine	Permanent Mauve

❶ Using Gamboge and Cadmium Orange, paint a star shape with a No. 8 brush. Leave white paper showing as highlights. Loosely form the flower shape. Whilst wet, drop in washes of Cadmium Orange and Burnt Sienna to create the centre and form on the petals.

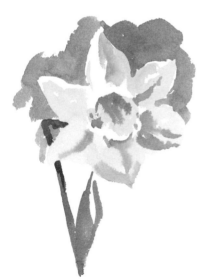

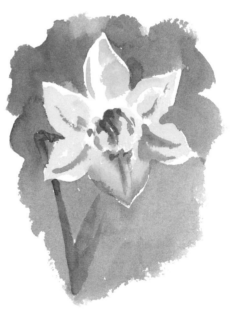

❷ Paint some single strokes of green (French Ultramarine and Gamboge) to represent a stem and a leaf. Make the petal overlap the stem. When dry, mix a flat wash of purple, (Cobalt Blue and Permanent Mauve) and paint the negative space.

❸ Continue your purple wash until a background forms and brings the flower forward. Enhance the centre with a few well-chosen darks. This exercise is a simple procedure and should be practised until you feel confident with the process.

Background first

If your subject matter is darker than the background it is possible to paint the background first then place the flowers on top. Remember to leave the background to dry before you start painting over the top.

❶ Use your No. 8 brush to paint a variegated wash of Cobalt Blue, Permanent Mauve and Naples Yellow to contrast with the red of the chrysanthemums. Try to keep your colour washes the same consistency as one another. Allow to dry.

❷ Paint the flowers in Cadmium Red and Alizarin Crimson directly onto the blue, letting some show through. Add the foliage with varying mixes of Cadmium Orange, French Ultramarine and Lemon Yellow. Drop in the flower centres with Cadmium Orange.

Cobalt Blue	Permanent Mauve	Naples Yellow	Cadmium Red
Alizarin Crimson	Cadmium Orange	Lemon Yellow	French Ultramarine

Leaving white space

If the flowers are lighter than the background you can still paint the background first by taking care to paint around them.

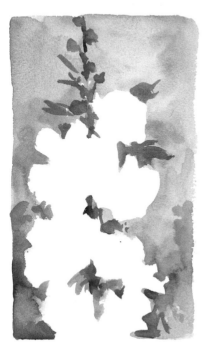

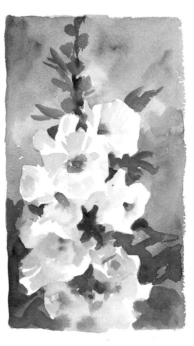

❶ With your No. 8 brush, use Ultramarine Violet, Coeruleum and Lemon Yellow to create the background and initial foliage, taking care to paint around the flower shapes. Start at the top apex and try to see how the white shapes connect with one another.

❷ With the background complete you can see more clearly what is needed with the flowers. Start by painting the centres Lemon Yellow and Cadmium Orange, ensuring you leave enough white paper. Pale washes of Ultramarine Violet help create the shadow areas.

Ultramarine Violet

Coeruleum

Lemon Yellow

Cadmium Orange

MUST KNOW

Keep your colours flowing

When painting backgrounds first it is important to keep your colours flowing. Using your wet-into-wet technique will help to keep your background cohesive and create a much more satisfying setting for your flowers.

Jigsaw painting

Jigsaw painting means slotting in the parts one piece at a time in any order you choose. This technique relies on the principle that the whole is greater than the sum of the individual parts. The idea is to slot the pieces together ad hoc and work quickly to create a sense of synchronicity.

❶ Start with the blues and pinks of the main flowers, keeping the shapes and colours very abstract in form.

❷ Working outwards, paint the negative shapes around the flowers with washes of Phthalo Blue, Burnt Sienna and Gamboge. Place more flowers and foliage randomly.

Phthalo
Blue

Burnt
Sienna

Gamboge

Permanent
Rose

Coeruleum

Naples
Yellow

Vermilion

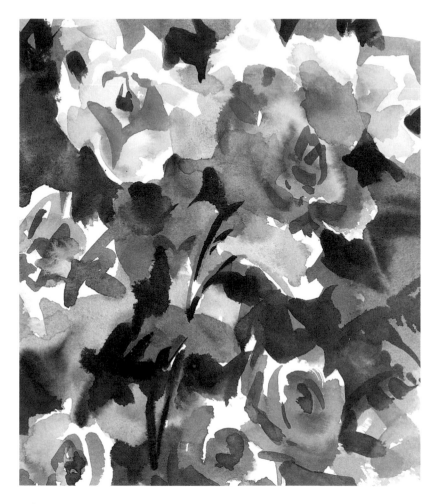

❸ Continuing with more of the same, put in smaller darks as accents in both flowers and background. Let your reactions take over and the painting will form itself.

MUST KNOW

Joining up the pieces

To paint in this way it is essential to keep the jigsaw pieces next to one another. Join each piece of paint together with another. In other words, do not place patches disparately across the paper and hope that they will join up later. The whole painting needs to evolve naturally. It is an organic process and in a way you are mimicking the way in which flowers grow and develop in nature. The painting will literally grow in front of your eyes.

▶ Flowers in containers

Painting flowers in containers can seem like a daunting task at first. What is a seemingly beautiful arrangement can become a painter's nightmare. A useful tip is to paint the flowers first and then add in the mass of foliage and pots around them. Remember that not everything needs to be clearly seen.

Geraniums

In the summer, pots of geraniums are a joy to paint. Their circular shapes and strong colours can seem complex at first; remember to simplify them.

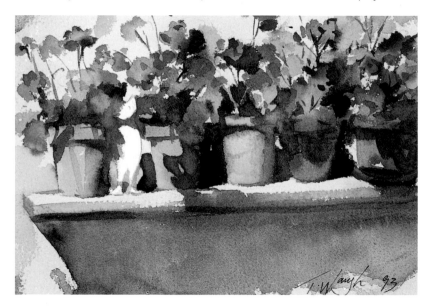

▲ This simple row of terracotta flowerpots filled with geraniums is in strong sunlight. The way the shadows and dark areas connect is vital to the painting's success.

MUST KNOW

Negative spaces

When painting flowers in containers, pay particular attention to the negative spaces, i.e. the spaces between the flowers and between the pots. This assists in an overall sense of depth.

Anemones

I saw these anemones in a friend's car and just had to paint them. All I had to hand to display them was a jam jar, but I love the simplicity of its shape.

Permanent Rose

Cobalt Blue

Cadmium Yellow

Phthalo Blue

Cadmium Orange

Coeruleum

Naples Yellow

Permanent Mauve

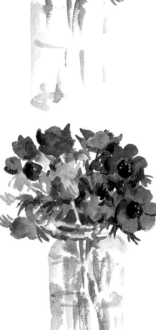

❶ Block in the flowers using washes of Permanent Rose and Cobalt Blue and a No. 8 brush. Mass in the foliage with Cadmium Yellow, Phthalo Blue and Cadmium Orange in a variegated wash, plus a few marks of Coeruleum to indicate the jar.

❷ Paint the stems using a dry brush. Vary the colours of the stems. Work the forms of the flowers with darker washes and add in some extra flowers. Use dots of Naples Yellow in the centres of the flowers.

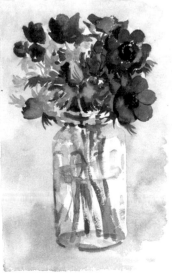

❸ When dry add any smaller accents to the flowers and foliage that may be required. Take pale washes of Cadmium Orange, Permanent Mauve, Cobalt Blue and Cadmium Yellow and paint in the background starting top left and working down to bottom right. Take care to stop your wash at the edge of the jar to complete the right-hand side.

Variety

As you look around, you will notice that all sorts of containers can be used for planting or displaying flowers, ranging from old tyres, boats and milk churns to the more usual vases and pots.

▲ The feeling of light in your paintings will enhance the view. The white of the paper is utilized here to represent the light hitting the subject.

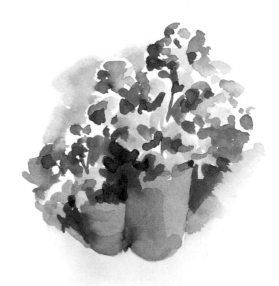

▶ Make some small studies of potted flowers. There is something very charming about red geraniums; they always seem to be so happy in their pots.

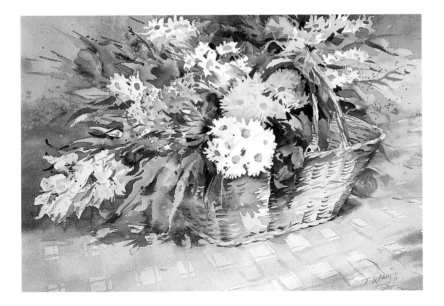

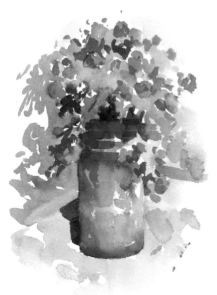

▲ Have fun picking and arranging summer flowers in a basket to show the abundance of the season and the sunlight that enlightens and illuminates everything.

◄ This rusty old milk churn made a great container for flowers that spill out and form their own designs and shadows.

MUST KNOW

Shadows

Look at how the shadows play an integral part between the flowers and their containers. The shadows are in recessed areas or cast by an external light source. These shadows create a three-dimensional effect.

Flowers in settings

Flowers are a constant reminder of the majesty of nature.
Whether you witness an entire nation of poppies spreading
their colour over fields, or the first daffodil of spring, they
stop you in your tracks and fill you with a sense of wonder.
Try to make these personal glimpses of flowers and their
settings inherent in your paintings.

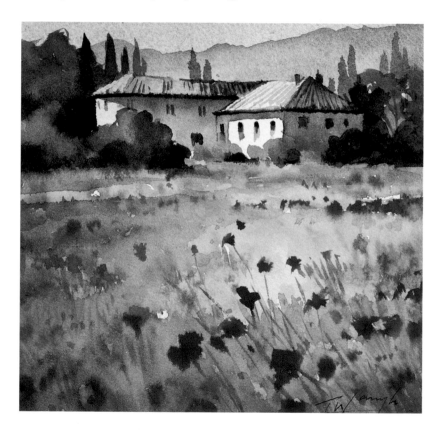

▲ Poppies in the South of France
18 x 18 cm (7 x 7 in)
The poppies in this field were mainly
painted wet-into-wet. The light on the
typically Provençal farmhouse serves to
enhance the colours.

▶ Val's Geraniums
25.5 x 20 cm (10 x 8 in)
This painting provided the opportunity to
study the light on pots of geraniums in a
deeply recessed window setting. The quality
of light is an important factor in creating a
sense of time and place.

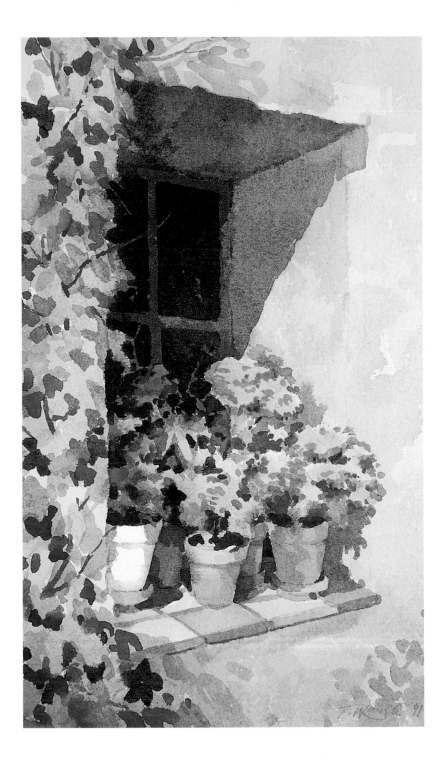

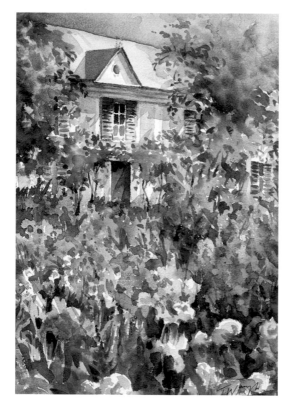

◄ Monet's Garden
35.5 x 25.5 cm (14 x 10 in).
It is a real joy to paint in
Monet's garden at Giverney
in Northern France. The
abundance of flowers and
the arrangement of colours
give the watercolour artist
so much inspiration.

► Nasturtiums
30.5 x 30.5 cm (12 x 12 in)
This square format seemed
appropriate for the diagonal
arrangement of nasturtiums.
The pot helps to offset the
composition and provides a
structure for this otherwise
loosely painted design.
Trailing flowers and foliage
enable you to explore
movement and colour.

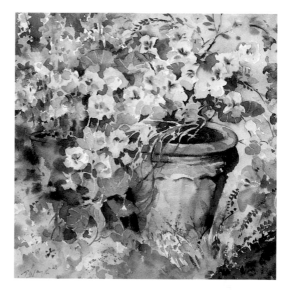

PAINTING FLOWERS

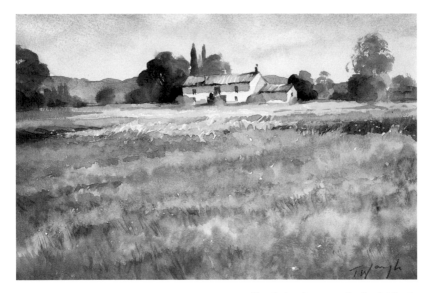

▲ Provençal Lavender
38 x 53 cm (15 x 21 in)
The main objective in this painting was to show the effects of large clumps of lavender spreading their colour over the flat fields of Provence. Instead of concentrating on the individual flowers, they were together in swathes of soft colour painted wet-into-wet.

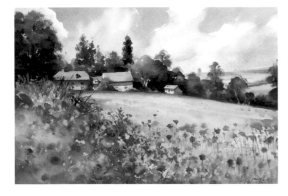

▲ Poppyfields at Great Barrington
37 x 53 cm (14½ x 21 in)
This painting is of a summer landscape in the Cotswolds. The poppies add a splash of colour to the foreground.

want to know more?

Take it to the next level...

Go to ...
▶ **Easy colour mixing** – page 20
▶ **Trees** – page 36
▶ **Shells and pebbles** – page 84

Other sources
▶ **Gardens**
   research new painting subjects
▶ **Bookclubs**
   specialist bookclubs, such as Artists' Choice
▶ **Art exhibitions**
   visit or even show your own work
▶ **Local venues**
   may allow you to display/sell your work
▶ **Publications**
   visit www.collins.co.uk for Collins art books

Need to know more?

There is a wealth of further information available for artists, particularly if you have access to the internet. Listed below are just some of the organizations or resources that you might find useful to help you to develop your watercolour painting.

Art Magazines
The Artist, Caxton House, 63/65 High Street, Tenterden, Kent TN30 6BD; tel: 01580 763673
www.theartistmagazine.co.uk
Artists & Illustrators, The Fitzpatrick Building, 188-194 York Way, London N7 9QR; tel: 020 7700 8500
International Artist, P. O. Box 4316, Braintree, Essex CM7 4QZ; tel: 01371 811345
www.artinthemaking.com
Leisure Painter, Caxton House, 63/65 High Street, Tenterden, Kent TN30 6BD; tel: 01580 763315
www.leisurepainter.co.uk

Art Materials
Daler-Rowney Ltd, Bracknell, Berkshire RG12 8ST; tel: 01344 424621
www.daler-rowney.com
Winsor & Newton, Whitefriars Avenue, Wealdstone, Harrow, Middlesex HA3 5RH; tel: 020 8427 4343
www.winsornewton.com

Art Shows
Artists & Illustrators Exhibition, The Fitzpatrick Building, 188-194 York Way, London N7 9QR; tel: 020 7700 8500 (for information and venue details)
Patchings Art, Craft & Design Festival, Patchings Art Centre, Patchings Farm, Oxton Road, Calverton, Nottinghamshire NG14 6NU; tel: 0115 965 3479
www.patchingsartcentre.co.uk

Art Societies
Federation of British Artists, Mall Galleries, 17 Carlton House Terrace, London SW1Y 5BD; tel: 020 7930 6844
www.mallgalleries.org.uk
Society for All Artists (SAA), P. O. Box 50, Newark, Nottinghamshire NG23 5GY; tel: 01949 844050
www.saa.co.uk

Bookclubs
Artists' Choice, P. O. Box 3, Huntingdon, Cambridgeshire PE28 0QX; tel: 01832 710201
www.artists-choice.co.uk

Internet Resources
Art Museum Network: the official website of the world's leading art museums
www.amn.org
Artcourses: an easy way to find part-time classes, workshops and painting holidays
www.artcourses.co.uk
The Arts Guild: on-line bookclub devoted to books on the art world
www.artsguild.co.uk
British Arts: useful resource to help you to find information about all art-related matters
www.britisharts.co.uk
British Library Net: comprehensive A-Z resource including 24-hour virtual museum/gallery
www.britishlibrary.net/museums.html
Galleryonthenet: provides member artists with gallery space on the internet
www.galleryonthenet.org.uk
Painters Online: interactive art club run by The Artist's Publishing Company
www.painters-online.com
WWW Virtual Library: extensive information on galleries worldwide
www.comlab.ox.ac.uk/archive/other/museums/galleries.html

Videos
APV Films, 6 Alexandra Square, Chipping Norton, Oxfordshire OX7 5HL; tel: 01608 641798
www.apvfilms.com
Teaching Art, P. O. Box 50, Newark, Nottinghamshire NG23 5GY; tel: 01949 844050
www.teachingart.com

Index

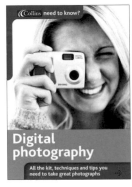
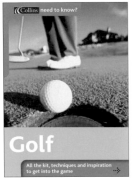
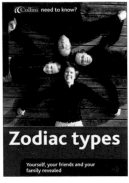
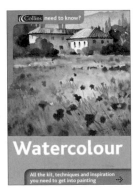